HISTORY AND HAUNTINGS
OF THE
HALLOWEEN CAPITAL

HISTORY AND HAUNTINGS
OF THE
HALLOWEEN CAPITAL

P

ROXY ORCUTT

NORTH STAR PRESS OF ST. CLOUD, INC.
St. Cloud, Minnesota

ISBN 978-0-87839-774-7

Printed in the United States of America

Published by
North Star Press of St. Cloud, Inc.
St. Cloud, MN

www.northstarpress.com

To my parents Don Leuthard and Debbie Seifermann,
for raising me to be a curious and open-minded person.

And to my husband Jim,
for being able to put up with that curious and open-minded person.

Table of Contents

A mural painted on the back on a business in Anoka. (Photo by Christy Urick.)

Introduction

The Halloween Honey's Paranormal Playground

MY MOTHER, DEBBIE, has worked in Anoka, Minnesota, for the last twenty-five years. When you work in Anoka for that long you are bound to encounter the Anoka Halloween Committee in some capacity. Mom certainly did! Her boss was heavily involved with the Anoka Halloween Committee for a time in the late 1990s. Mom helped out when she could with bookkeeping duties and whatnot for the committee. One day after school when I was fourteen or fifteen, I found myself hanging out at Mom's work. The Anoka Halloween Committee had received letters from an elementary school in Kansas asking why Anoka, Minnesota, was called The Halloween Capital of the World. Mom's boss spotted me perched next to her desk, looking bored, and tasked me with answering these children. How fun! My first writing gig!

The letters from the kids were sweet, handwritten in that large-lettered, soft-penciled style on wide-lined paper, mandatory for elementary school student adorableness. I wrote two letters that afternoon. First, I answered the children correctly. I told them the tale of the 1920 organization and mounting of a city-wide celebration on Halloween night to keep kids out of trouble. My second letter, the one I was going to show to my mom's boss as a joke, was downright evil. Quite literally. I made up a story about how Anoka was founded by devil worshippers and as time went on the town folks had to be more secretive about their Satanic dalliances, so they regulated one night a year, Halloween night, to celebrate their dark lord. The big secret was that Anoka's founders were going to pass this off as some innocent festival to the rest of the nation and thus was born Anoka, Minnesota: The Halloween Capital of the World.

I amused myself more than anyone else with the second letter. My mom read it and rolled her eyes as she handed it back to me with a scoff; clearly she was used to my smart-aleck behavior at that point. Her boss met the second letter with the same head-shaking style. Obviously, that letter was not sent to the schoolchildren in Kansas, but I think that day was pivotal for me. It was then that the festival I loved so, so much—the Anoka Halloween Celebration—truly captured my imagination. I was always in awe of the celebration as a small child, but at that particular age, the undesirable, awkward, in-your-own-head-everything-is-lame age of mid-adolescence, I felt something was not so lame. Mockable, clearly, but not uncool.

In these past fifteen years or so I have written about Anoka a lot. There were jokey "memos" to my fellow co-workers at my first office job, in which I cracked jokes about Anoka, the townspeople, and Halloween. I tried my hand at fiction about Anoka and the Halloween celebration, pages and pages of writings about the town and Halloween. I can't think of a time since that day so many years ago where I didn't want to write about Anoka and Halloween. Or not talk about it. Or not experience it. The spirit of Anoka Halloween caught me that day and it hasn't let go since.

The city of Anoka has always been a part of my childhood tapestry; I think that is why it is so magical to me. I still see the town through a child's eyes.

I didn't grow up in Anoka. Rather, I grew up in a rural town about twenty-five minutes north, called Oak Grove. I think that's why I might see it so differently than those who have grown up here. Anoka was a special place for and my heart has always been here. My mom's work was where I would spend summer days and afternoons after school ever since I was in kindergarten. My aunt Carla, uncle John and cousin Adam have lived in Anoka my whole life. Their house was a second home to my sister Cori and I growing up. I thought their house was everything a house The Halloween Capital of the World should be: an old house from the 1920s, refinished, with whispers about a ghost haunting the bathroom off the hallway; two black cats, Susie and Cleo, who were the two witchiest cats I've ever known; and Carla's kitchen corkboard filled with years and years of Anoka Halloween buttons. I would sometimes just stand in front of the corkboard and pick out my favorite design, which seemed to change each time I gazed at the board.

I couldn't believe how easy it was to walk to places in Anoka. Oak Grove was so rural and I lived on a dirt road. Anoka had sidewalks and shops and rivers. And the best part, Anoka had witches and pumpkins everywhere you turned, all year long.

To me, Anoka was magic.

Now, I understand what that magic is: it's history, rivers, beautiful homes, industrious people. It's that little something special, something indescribable.

It's something supernatural.

My first true memory of a Halloween night in Anoka was one of the most memorable Halloweens in years, for not only myself but for the entire state of Minnesota.

I experienced Halloween like any other kid growing up in the Midwest. The weeks-long planning of costumes, the fresh plastic smell when trying it on for the first time (my mother was not crafty, so we bought our Halloween costumes) the magic of transforming into not only another person for a night, but into something scary. I was always something scary. I never went for that princess stuff when I was a little girl. I knew what Halloween was for, and it was to be scary.

I never could be in my full costume at the school Halloween party, though. Being scary always required an elaborate make-up job and we didn't have that kind of time in the morning before school. I was a little disappointed, but I did get to go full-bore on Halloween night. One of my favorite Halloween costumes as a kid was from when I was eight years old in 1991.

Nearly every Minnesotan can tell you where they were on Halloween night in 1991. That night just over twenty-eight inches of snow was dumped on the Twin Cities, with no end in sight.

The morning started out typically. Dad left early for work, Mom was going to drop me and my sister Cori off at school with our costumes in tow for our classroom parties, Cori being three grades ahead of me. Me, Mom and Cori then planned to go to Carla's house in Anoka that night for trick-or-treating with Adam.

I was a witch that year, with a green face and everything. I remember I was so excited because Mom let me bring my make-up to school and trusted me to apply it all by myself, and I did an awesome job of it. The classroom party got started in the afternoon and I was so pleased with how wicked I looked.

The day ended and with bags of candy in hand, Cori and I met up after school and waited for Mom to pick us up. We climbed into the back of her car, a two-door 1989 black Camero, and made a quick dash home for something. I don't remember what we needed at home, but I remember it had started snowing. Minutes later we were on the road heading to Anoka. The snow was falling so heavily by then, cars seemed to be sliding everywhere. Mom was using colorful language as she did her best to transport us safely to our destination in her little sports car. I was clueless as all get out as to what was happening, still happy as a clam in my witch costume.

We finally reached Carla's house and Cori and I bounded inside to see Adam. Mom trudged in behind us and spent quite a bit of time talking to her sister in the kitchen.

Eventually, the adults came into the living room and Mom told me if I wanted to go trick-or-treating, I had to wear a different costume. I was very annoyed. I looked so good and spooky! Apparently it had something to do with a thin vinyl dress and cape not being warm enough to wear in a blizzard trick-or-treating. I didn't want to miss out on the candy so I begrudgingly changed into the only costume available for me to wear, Adam's Halloween costume from the previous year. Not only was it a boy's costume, it was also way too big for me since Adam was three years older than me. It was a jester costume and quite warm. Fine, I'd wear it.

Cori, who was a cat that year since she was a cat for Halloween every year, and Adam, who was a dead hockey player (of course) and I bundled up, along with Mom and Carla, and headed out to the neighborhoods around their house. It was an absolute blast. People were thrilled to open their doors to such steadfast trick-or-treaters. The kids in Anoka were out in droves that night, too, with a lot of unhappy looking parents dragging their feet behind them in the never-ending snow.

With cold cheeks and running noses, we kids got back to Carla's house and changed out of our wet Halloween costumes and into warm pajamas. By the time we got home from trick-or-treating, my uncle John had gotten home from work and Mom got on the phone with Dad. After a short chat it was settled. Me, Cori and Mom were going to have to spend the night at Carla's house. The snow showed no sign of stopping and Mom couldn't risk driving us home in her little "gutless" car.

We kids were thrilled! We loved having sleepovers with Adam, especially at Carla's house! They seemed to have an endless collection of movies. Mom and Carla exchanged uneasy glances as they watched us tear down the hallway to select a movie to watch that night. The uneasiness wasn't due to the fact that there were going to be three children all hopped up on candy and snow in the house overnight, it was the fact that there were going to be three children all hopped up on candy and snow in the house for . . . who knew how long. The snow showed no sign of stopping and Carla wasn't exactly prepared for extended overnight guests.

To get their minds off of what might lay ahead for the next few days, Mom suggested to Carla that they should meet up with her co-workers, who were celebrating Halloween night at the American Legion on Main Street in downtown Anoka. Uncle John was happy to stay home with us kids, and Mom and Carla wasted no time disappearing into the snowy Halloween night.

Only long after Cori, Adam and I had gone to bed did Mom and Carla return, driven home by some brave, sober souls in the thick of the storm. I later heard that Mom only fell once walking back into the house.

We were stuck at Aunt Carla's house in Anoka until it stopped snowing, which wasn't until November 3. When Mom's car could finally be shoveled out and the roads were clear to drive on, we sped away from Carla's house as fast as we could. While we kids thought it was a wonderful surprise vacation, Mom and Carla needed a break from each other.

My dad seemed to be the only one who truly enjoyed the snow. Even though he had to shovel and snowplow, he got to spend three days forced off of work in the house with just the dogs. Staycation!

The Halloween Blizzard of 1991 ended up dropping 28.4 inches of snow on the Twin Cities metro area.

P

I WAS IN NO HURRY to leave Carla's house so many years ago, and I came back and now make my own home in Anoka. I work in downtown Anoka and I can direct you to any park in this city. I am an active and involved citizen who speaks at city council meetings and tell my friends and family to "shop local." I write about Anoka almost daily on my blog "The Halloween Honey," and the response has been wonderful. Not only from the city itself, but from the citizens of Anoka who go out of their way to meet me and tell me they love the city as much as I do.

I have turned The Halloween Capital of the World into my paranormal playground over the last few years. There is something in the air here; the supernatural current that runs through the area makes me want to find out as much as I can about this mysterious and spooky little town.

I chose to start with the history of Anoka's claim to fame, the title of "The Halloween Capital of the World." How on earth did this little community grab such a grandiose title?

From there, I wanted to know what made this town so spooky. Luckily, I already knew all the ghost stories, from my time as a docent for the Anoka County Historical Society's Ghosts of Anoka tour.

In the late summer of 2011, I was looking for more opportunities to get out of the house. My daughter was going to be turning one in November and I was pretty happy to have made it through her infancy successfully as a stay-at-home mom. While I was working very part-time at Party Papers and Costumes in downtown Anoka (more on this place later), I needed a little something more. I decided instead of trying to find additional employment, I would volunteer. Where did I volunteer? Being the history dork I am, I took my free time to the Anoka County Historical Society.

The Anoka County Historical Society is a great resource right in downtown Anoka. It is also home to the Ghosts of Anoka tour, led by citizens knowledgeable about history and hauntings in The Halloween Capital. Not only do they know their stuff, they also wear beautiful costumes while conducting the tours. These docents, as they are known, deck themselves out in costumes representing the era Anoka was founded, the late 1800s. I love a good costume, and I love an even better reason to wear one.

I went to my informational volunteer meeting with the Historical Society with the mindset that Ghosts of Anoka tour had all the docents they would need. Why would such a great program be in need of volunteers to lead the tour? Surely, they must have a waiting list of people eager to jump at the chance of leading the tour. Of course I secretly hoped this wasn't true. While I was happy to do whatever the Historical Society needed me to do—stuff envelopes, re-shelve books, anything—I was secretly hoping to be a docent.

Imagine my thrill when I met with Elaine, the volunteer coordinator at the Anoka County Historical Society, and she told me that a docent for the ghost tour had decided they couldn't do it. Oh, boy, did my ears perk up. "I mean, sure . . . if that's what you need me to do," I told her. I was trying to play it cool, but I was beyond excited! That very day I was armed with a script and an appointment to shadow another tour in the next coming weeks. I went home on cloud nine.

Before too long, however, reality set in. I am not a great public speaker. I never have been. I get nervous, talk too fast and laugh inappropriately. I wanted to do a good job leading the Ghosts of Anoka tour because it was something I loved so much and I wanted others to enjoy it just as much as me. I didn't want people walking away from the tour talking about the awkward docent.

Securing a good costume was no problem. I turned to Party Papers and Costumes, of course, and found a one-of-a-kind piece made by one of our former employees who was also a costumer. It was a Civil War-era style dress made for an actress in a stage show. Problem was, this actress had very strange proportions. The shop had a hard time selling the costume because no one fit into it. The skirt was quite large, but the top was pretty tight. I tried the piece on, taken with the bustles on the back of the skirt, and was going to make it work. I brought it to my mother-in-law and she made it fit like a glove. Let's just say, my mother-in-law has an entire room in her house dedicated to sewing. She knows her stuff.

I was all set. I knew my script, the walking route, I had the costume and I was ready to shadow the more experienced docent. I was psyched out at the last second by Mary, the owner of Party Papers and Costumes, of all people. "Don't forget," she told me, trying to be encouraging, "it's a performance." At that moment my brain shut down. I don't do "performance." "Performance" meant a stage, and lights, and worst of all, an audience.

At this point, I had been on a few Ghosts of Anoka tours, and while the majority of people are engaged in the tour, asking questions and being marveled by the spooky stories, there are the few on the tour who light up a cigarette and trail away from the group, play on their phones the entire tour or even show up to the tour three sheets to the wind. All these potential issues that may arise while conducting a tour, while also speaking in front of a group of people, seeped into my head. How on earth was I going to get a group of twenty-five drunk people playing on their phones across busy Main Street?! Of course, that was a worst-case-scenario that has never happened.

I shadowed the more experienced docent and it went pretty smoothly. I told a few of the stories, reading from my script and talking like it was a race. Oof. The docent was kind and told me I did a wonderful job.

A few weeks passed and an email was sent out to all the docents asking if they were available to take a tour on a upcoming Saturday night. I took the tour. I figured I needed to stop wasting the Historical Society's time and do what I said I would do. A few days later, Elaine called me.

"I just wanted you to be aware that the group you are taking out on Saturday night is a group of special needs adults," she told me. "Are you okay with that?"

Was I ever! I told her I was even more excited, which may have come across as kind of strange, but I didn't care. This, like the other tours, had the potential of turning into a disaster, but it also had to potential to be amazing, and amazing it was.

I took my tour, which was about twenty-five people from a group home as well as a few group home employees, on the haunted tour around downtown Anoka, and I had one of the best times of my life. They were an enthusiastic, curious and engaged bunch. Never once did I look into the crowd and see someone with a bored expression or looking at a phone. It was bliss.

I even got to hear a handful of ghost stories from the group members themselves, which were so wonderfully entertaining.

After that tour, I knew I couldn't top it. I would get clammy hands just thinking about leading another tour and the closer Halloween came the busier Party Papers and Costumes got, and I needed to be there.

The Historical Society understood. I had wanted to try it, and I did, and they were lovely enough to grant me the opportunity.

Since telling the stories of Anoka'a haunted history and Halloween as a docent for the Anoka County Historical Society wasn't for me, I am writing this book instead. I learned a lot working with the Historical Society and from being a living, breathing member of Anoka's past while volunteering. I want to share my passion and knowledge for this town and explore why it seems to be such a hotbed for paranormal activity.

Does the Halloween Capital title and the spirits that haunt the city of Anoka have anything to do with each other? Or is it purely coincidence that this haunted hamlet is called The Halloween Capital of the World?

In this book you will read about the history of Halloween in Anoka, as well as some of the more spirited stories about the haunted locations that played a role in the creation of the Halloween Capital of the World. A few of my personal experiences are thrown into the mix.

All those years I tried my hand at making up stories about The Halloween Capital of the World was a waste of time. The real thing was more interesting than anything I could have dreamed up.

(Photo by Christy Urick.)

One

Welcome to The Halloween Capital of the World

THE ENTIRE HALLOWEEN Capital of the World exists within a seven-mile radius of upper Midwestern soil.

The holiday of Halloween is deeply rooted in ancient European history and is celebrated as a holy day by pagan and earth-based religious around the world to this day. October 31 conjures up images of witches, ghosts and all things spooky for nearly every nation around the world. This holiday, which started halfway across the world, was brought to the United States by early settlers to New England and spread west along with the rest of the nation. In the United States today, Halloween is second only to Christmas in holiday popularity. This unique worldwide holiday steeped in tradition, magic, and ancient ritual has its entire world capital, declared by the U.S. Congress, in Anoka, Minnesota, population of roughly 18,000.

The city of Anoka, Minnesota, has been described in many different ways by many different people. A modern-day village on all accounts, this northern suburb of Minneapolis has for the most part been able to avoid all the trappings of the strip-mall, chain-store, cookie-cutter neighborhoods that have overtaken the suburbs. This is by design. These chain stores and big box retailers are planted in cities just outside Anoka, peeking in. Anoka's geography allows its unique and antiquated community style. Being nestled between two rivers, the Mississippi and the Rum, gives the city a feeling of seclusion and a bit of protection from the outside world. Down the center of town runs an honest-to-goodness pedestrian-friendly Main Street, where shops and restaurants sit snugly together doing business in 100-year-old brick buildings. Anoka, also being the county seat, shares its old-fashioned Main Street with a large courthouse and jail that bring thousands of people into town for work and other county-related purposes every weekday, creating a bustling mini-metropolitan atmosphere.

A few blocks north of Main Street is Jackson Street, a one-stop watering hole peppered with six bars and pubs all on the same block, making for an easy night of partying. When leaving the street for the night visitors are greeted with the somber, serious courthouse at the end of Jackson Street staring down, a reminder to not drink and drive, or do anything else stupid.

Tattoo parlors, an organic grocer and a yoga studio draw a more alternative crowd into town on weekends. Many cafés, several antique shops, a successful community theater and a stellar costume shop bring many more people into town for these destination locations any day of the week.

Out from Main Street shoot the avenues and sidewalks where the neighborhoods and schools lay. Numbered streets, streets named for presidents and prominent Anoka citizens of the past make up the rest of Anoka. Homes as old as 170 years stand beside homes built throughout the twentieth century in Anoka's neighborhoods. In the center of town, surrounded by these neighborhoods, sits Goodrich Field, a large football field where the Anoka Tornados high school football team plays on Friday nights.

The city of Anoka is part storybook Americana as well as part government-sanctioned mental healthcare provider for the last 114 years. Aside from the large government center, the courthouse and jail, along the river heading south into the city of Champlin is a row of rehabilitation centers and group homes. A large, red-bricked state asylum from the nineteenth century (being used today as a drug and alcohol treatment center) is clear across town from the rehab homes near the railroad.

A high school, a middle school and three elementary schools, some as old as the town itself, take care of the education of the children of Anoka. Parks, promenades along the river, public and private docks and an ice rink keep modern Anoka citizens outside year-round. The majority of the citizens have walking accessibility to nearly everything in town.

If you were to ask any Anoka citizen what the town's identity was, they would tell you, "Halloween."

Ask another few citizens what the town's identity would be and they would tell you, "the ghosts."

Everywhere you go in Anoka there seems to be a ghost story lurking. Someone lives in a haunted house or knows someone who does. Their place of business is haunted or could have sworn they saw a ghost the other night while walking through the park. Anoka is a haunted city. There is no doubt about that.

Two

The Land of Ghosts

THERE IS NO ONE WAY to find a ghost. The scientific method all but has to be thrown out the window when it comes to proof of the spirit world. What someone may see out of the corner of their eye or capture for a split second on a video recorder may never ever be duplicated or happen exactly the same way again.

Some scientific thought is applied to studying the supernatural. Those who search out proof of ghosts have been able to find some elements in the earth that cause hauntings by their nature alone. One such school of thought is called the Limestone Theory.

The Limestone Theory suggests that the naturally occurring geological formation of limestone is a conductor for energy. According to some in the paranormal field, as limestone decays and falls apart, it gives off an unusually high energy level on a popular tool used in paranormal investigating, an EMF detector. An EMF detector—EMF being an acronym for electromagnetic field—detects the energy given off by electrically charged objects. This constantly dispersing energy acts as somewhat of a magnet for the departed who haven't left the earth. When a haunting is taking place, the spirit requires energy to manifest itself. This energy can come from the energy of a living person, the batteries in a camera or a naturally occurring element. According to those who have studied it, limestone is one such element. Spirits are drawn to lime-stone and in some cases *stuck* because of the limestone, forced to stay around because of it.

It just so happens that the city of Anoka is built on top of limestone.

Another piece of information brought to us by the paranormal investigating world is the belief that spirits cannot cross flowing waters. Some say that this particular theory comes from the Bible. According to the below scripture:,

> When the unclean spirit is gone out of man, he walketh through dry places, seeking rest, finding none.
>
> (Matthew 12:43)

According to Haunted Orange County, a paranormal group out of California, this is more in reference to a demon. A demon, after being cast out of a human, can find no rest on dry land, there-fore chooses to rest in the water. When the ghost of a human comes upon water, all they see are cast-out demons. They choose then not to cross the water out of fear.

Incidentally, the city of Anoka is surrounded by two large, flowing rivers.

People came to Anoka, lived in Anoka, died in Anoka and stayed in Anoka. It seems that they have been drawn here by the spirit of community, the spirit of hard work and industry, the spirit of care and comfort. It seems the spirit of Halloween was destined to come to this river city all along.

Anoka has nine locations of the National Registry of Historic Places alone, as well as 130 other buildings, homes and places of business built in the late 1800s and throughout the 1900s that are considered to be historic by the city of Anoka Community Plan on Historic Preservation. Anoka was born and raised with boundless energy. The town has been filled with industrious people who created, built and sold what they made, compassionate people who cared for the ill and led by people who didn't think it was too much for this little town on the river to become the entire world's capital of Halloween.

It's no surprise that some of the people who made Anoka what it is today are in no hurry to leave. Whether or not they were in this city before the Halloween Capital title, made their mark during that time, or came and saw the town well after, the spirits that haunt Anoka are here to stay.

To better understand what kind of energy and spirit built this haunted and historic city, we have to start at the beginning and explore Anoka before this little piece of Minnesota was called The Halloween Capital of the World.

Three

On Both Sides:
A Brief History of Anoka Before 1920

THE LAND BETWEEN the Mississippi River and Rum River that is now Anoka, Minnesota, began as a neutral territory between the Native American Dakota and Ojibwa tribes. Common ground was found on this spot after a brief encounter between the two tribes that initially ran the Dakota (the original occupants of the land) across the Mississippi into the modern-day city of Champlin. Soon after the skirmish an agreement was reached between the tribes and the land was used equally by both. That spirit of cooperation lends to the name "Anoka," a combination of the Dakota and Ojibwa languages—more specifically, a combination of the Dakota word *a-no-ka-tan-han*, meaning "on both sides of the river," and the Ojibwa word *on-o-kay*, meaning "working waters."

In 1680, French explorer and Catholic priest Father Louis Hennepin came across the land now known as Anoka. However, no settlers came to stay until one hundred and sixty years later. Once the settlers came, the town quickly boomed.

Settled in 1844, Anoka was the hub for all manner of trading and traveling among the other states and territories. Within six years time the city even boasted a flour mill, a woodworking plant and a school. However, Minneapolis was settled in 1856, putting a timetable on Anoka's relevance in the trading industries. The same year, Anoka established a ferry system across the Mississippi River to make for easier travel between Anoka and the neighboring city of Champlin. Ten years later, a rail system was set up between Minneapolis and Chicago, making Anoka's water-based way of travel seem outdated. Business now mostly came through Minneapolis, leaving Anoka behind when it came to the industries it dominated in its first few years of existence. Despite this, the city remained a diligent contributor to the milling and logging industry.

After the blow the city took once the Minneapolis-Chicago rail was established, it seemed Anoka couldn't catch a break. A series of fires popped up throughout town between the years of 1855 and 1884, forcing large chunks of the burgeoning city, previously built mostly out of wood, to be rebuilt in 1884 with more resilient brick materials.

In keeping with Anoka's less-than-ideal luck of the nineteenth century, by 1885, logging, the town's main source of income, was beginning to dwindle. In 1886, a potato starch factory opened and Anoka became an unlikely superstar in potato production. A shoe factory was also brought into the town, employing hundreds of people and producing up to eight hundred pairs of shoes a day. By 1898, another industry was brought to Anoka by the state of Minnesota. A state hospital was to be built, the First State Asylum for the Insane. The hospital opened in 1899.

The unlikely combination of shoes, potatoes and the mentally ill remained Anoka's big business for the early part of the 1900s. That year, Anoka's population had reached 3,769 and farming towns were beginning to pop up around the city, bringing more children into the city's schools, and befriending more of Anoka's children. As true as it is today, when groups of unsupervised kids get together, trouble seems to follow.

The Rum River in Anoka. (Photo by Christy Urick.)

Four

Michief and Mayhem

FOR MOST CHILDREN in the early decades of the twentieth century, Halloween was a night for troublemaking. The children of Anoka and their friends from the surrounding communities took this idea to a whole new level. It wasn't so much what the kids themselves did, it was more the destruction that followed in the wake of their actions that concerned the town. Anoka's youth and their mischief are best illustrated in an essay written by Jay Dugan in 1952 for *The Ford Reader*:

On the morning after Halloween, 1919, early risers in Anoka, MN were greeted by an astonishing sight. Cows, it seemed, had taken over the town!

Bovines were browsing everywhere. They were looking soulfully into the store windows, calmly eating flowers from window boxes, and strolling up Main Street singly and in pairs. Two were bawling lustily in the city lock-up and another was sleeping soundly in the sheriff's office. One deep-chested milker, hungry for knowledge, meandered through the high school digesting information at a great rate. When found, she had eaten her way to Madagascar on the globe of the world.

A dismantled carriage the morning of November 1—a Halloween prank from the night before. (Photo courtesy of ABC Newspaper.)

Letting cows free in the middle of the night was one of the many pranks the kids of Anoka liked to pull on Halloween night, along with soaped windows, taking apart carriages only to reassemble them on rooftops, and the dreaded outhouse tipping. This seemed to be one of the kids favorite pranks to play on their unsuspecting neighbors on Halloween night. There is a tale of Dagger Dan of Champlin who was described as a gruff, large man people went out of their way to avoid. But not the children of Anoka on Halloween night. As Dagger Dan entered his outhouse for a nighttime bathroom break, a group of kids tipped the outhouse, rolling Dagger Dan down a hill. He came out of the outhouse at the bottom of the hill physically unscathed. There is no record of the children who pulled this prank being identified, or if Dagger Dan ever got his much-wanted revenge.

It all seems very cute and harmless today, but these incidents were big problems for the people of Anoka in the 1900s, so much so that a few citizens began to arm themselves in preparation of Halloween night. Halloween seemed to bring out the worst in the town and its kids: the adults on edge, anticipating what the morning of November 1 would bring, and the kids planning ways to top the year before in their bad behavior. Halloween and the children of Anoka were becoming a toxic mix.

By 1919, things were beginning to change. The cow debacle set into motion the change that would put Anoka, Minnesota, on its way to holding the title of The Halloween Capital of the World.

Five

The Formative Years
of Anoka Halloween

"For so many years that no one knows when it started, it has been accepted as writ and dogma that Hallowe'en should be celebrated, on the part of the older folks, by sedate parties and 'at homes'; on the part of the children by theft of gateposts and the tincanning of the professor's house."

(Anoka Herald, *November 1, 1921*)

I N THE EARLY 1920S, the town and citizens of Anoka were flourishing as a suburb of Minneapolis and optimistic about their future. Business was booming, security and comfort were all around and the sense of community was strong thanks to ambitious and tenacious citizens—despite what went on during Halloween night

P

George Green:
The Man Behind Anoka Halloween

In 1920, Anoka's population was well beyond 4,000 and the town was enjoying steady growth in its industries and wealth. Anoka was producing and drawing in doctors, lawyers and judges. These prestigious folks were proud to call Anoka their home. The majority of the families of the well-to-do lived on Third Avenue, making that particular street one of the most desirable address in town.

The First State Asylum for the Insane, one of the biggest employers in town, was rebranded as the Anoka State Asylum and was now used to house female patients only. The "Anoka" potato was being shipped to every state in the union. The shops on Main Street continued to flourish and serve Anoka and its outlying communities. The locally owned shops and other businesses had formed a Commercial Club years prior to help foster business-community relationships. In 1920, the president of this club was a man named George Green.

George Green was a true son of Anoka. Born within the city limits in October of 1879 to real estate and insurance man Clarence Green and his wife Sadie, he and his sister, Ethel, were raised on State Street in Anoka near the Mississippi River. When George first struck out on his own he went into the meat business, but quickly found he was better suited to the family industry of real estate. He joined his father's business in 1901, rechristening the business as C.D. Green and Son. In 1904, at the age of twenty-five, George married local girl Dorothy Bruns. The next year he was a father to daughter Eleanor. George wasn't the richest man in town, but he was among the most liked and respected.

ANNOUNCEMENT!
Get Ready for the Largest and Best

HALLOWE'EN CELEBRATION

Ever put on in Anoka

TUESDAY EVENING, OCT. 31

Bring the whole family and let's celebrate together. Watch next week's papers for further details.

An *Anoka Union* ad from 1920 adverting Anoka's first Halloween celebration. (Courtesy of ABC Newspaper.)

George was the definition of an involved citizen in Anoka. Along with being a member, then president of the Commercial Club, George also belonged to the Kiwanis Club of Anoka, the Knights of Pythias, the Ancient Order of United Workmen, and the Anoka Golf Club, and was very involved with his church, the Baptist Church of Anoka.

P

AFTER THE COW INCIDENT of Halloween 1919 was long gone but not forgotten, in September of 1920 the citizens of Anoka turned to influential men in the community to see how to best avoid a repeat of the previous year's trouble. George Green was among this group of high profile men. George, along with his other members of the Commercial Club, suggested to the town that they stage an organized event for all the children to attend. The city had Halloween events and an annual dance at the Anoka Armory, but that was strictly for adults, featuring a jazz band from Minneapolis and seventy-five cents in admission per couple. A Halloween committee was formed, primarily made up of the members of the Commercial Club. If the men in Anoka in the 1900s liked anything, they liked a well-organized group to belong to. George volunteered to head up the committee. By the time the planning stages were underway, the Halloween Committee had collected three hundred dollars from local merchants to stage the celebration for Halloween night.

On October 20, 1920, an article about the upcoming event ran in the *Anoka Herald*:

> Anoka Hallowe'en Party
> On Saturday evening, Oct. 30, every man, woman and child in Anoka and neighboring farm communities are expected to take part in a novel party which will be held on our own downtown.

Everything that goes to make a real, old-fashioned hilarious Halloween party will be in order. Music by the famous Fireman's Band of Minneapolis, jack-o-lanterns and costume parade by schools, contest and games on the street.

The committee in charge has arranged to have a generous supply of fun and fun-making equipment, confetti, etc., on sale so everyone may enter into the spirit of the occasion with plenty of pep. The business houses will be decorated in keeping with the occasion. Watch their windows for contests and prizes. Remember, this is your party so don't forget to turn out and keep things lively in our first community Hallowe'en party.

It was framed not so much as a request for the people of Anoka to attend the first Halloween celebration, but more that it was their responsibility to attend. The celebration was a success. The first Anoka Halloween Parade lasted ten minutes, and included five hundred people marching from Bridge Square down Main Street with the Minneapolis Fire Department Band playing. Directly after the parade a wagon of apples, nuts and other treats was wheeled down Main Street along the parade route and distributed to all who attended. Directly after the parade, a large bonfire was held in town and most turned out to warm up and snack on their treats. Like years previous, a dance was held at the armory that night. Apparently, the addition of a parade, a bonfire and street fair-like atmosphere on Halloween night was enough to deter Anoka's youth from causing trouble.

Two days later, a rave review of the First Annual Halloween Celebration was printed in the *Anoka Herald*:

> Everyone Joined In The Hallowe'en Celebration Saturday Evening
>
> The *Herald* does not know who suggested the Hallowe'en stunt that was pulled off Saturday evening on the downtown streets of Anoka, but we do know that it was an unqualified success in its inception [. . .] Everyone except the dead, sick, and lame were there and joined in the harmless revelry.

The first Anoka Halloween committee basked in their success and prepared to aim even higher the next year. Planning stages began much sooner than September for the 1921 celebration, realizing it would take more than a month to top the first year's triumph. Word of Anoka's first Halloween celebration and its success spread quickly throughout the neighboring cities. George Green was appointed president of the Halloween Committee again for 1921 and new events were added, one of the most popular being a window decorating contest for the local merchants. The 1921 Anoka Halloween celebration grew by leaps and bounds.

From the *Anoka Union*, November 2, 1921:

> Ten Thousand In Celebration
>
> Anoka enjoys best community affair in its history.
>
> Anoka had ten thousand people on its streets celebrating Hallowe'en Saturday night, and Anoka had more than that. She had the biggest community get-together in her history.
>
> Last year the plan was tried to have a municipal community celebration, and thus give the boys and girls a good time and leave it to their honor not to

commit depredations as had been done for so many years. The plan worked well.

The plan did a lot of things that have proved a good one. It brought Anoka thousands of visitors, it made an appearance any city could be proud of, and it advertised us far and near.

The *Anoka Herald* took more of a poetic approach in describing the Second Annual Anoka Halloween Celebration. From the November 1, 1921 edition:

Last night, there were 10,000 people on the streets of Anoka. Confetti filled the air; long serpentines twined from passing cars. Masks and costumes were everywhere. Three bands played at once in the downtown district. Every store was lighted and decorated; every place was filled with interested visitors.

[. . .] Sidewalks were so crowded as to be almost impassable. The parade was late, but if it had started on time it could never have got through the streets. Finally, at 8:00 p.m. the bands blared out, and the fête was formally opened by 1,200 shouting, dancing men and women and children. The Hayseed band led off. Then Anoka's Boy Scouts, in full uniform, clicking at route step, with merit badges on their arms and "Boy Scouts! Rah!" on their lips.

And then came the king of the Fiji Isles. There were witches and clowns and soldiers and clowns.

Forty-five nurses from the state hospital for the insane followed.

And after that were more school children—so many that nobody even tried to count them."

The Halloween Committee had staged young women on street corners throughout the parade route selling noise makers and confetti at a "nominal price."

The sales of the party favors were not to recoup the cost of the festival, but rather, "We figured that any help we could give the celebration would mean just that much more fun," as George Green told the *Minneapolis Journal*.

P

Sudden Death of George Green Saddens Community

George Green's obituary. (Courtesy of ABC Newspaper.)

ALTHOUGH HE MAINTAINED the title of vice president through the 1930s and 1940s, 1921 would be the final year George Green served as president of the Halloween Committee. Halloween wouldn't be the only thing George Green's legacy left for Anoka. By the end of his life George owned several businesses and homes in the city, along with a theater and many other pieces of Anoka property. At the time of his death, George Green had held the unfortunate title of being the city's most popular pallbearer, having served as pallbearer at more funerals in the city of Anoka than any other person. When George Green passed away in October of 1947, all the businesses in Anoka closed for his funeral and hundreds of people attended the service and lined the streets to say farewell to George. Fittingly enough, George Green was buried at Forest Hills Cemetery in Anoka on October 31, 1947.

Six

Forest Hills Cemetery and the Gray Ghost

W HILE NO ONE HAS claimed to see the spirit of Anoka Halloween, King George Green, roam the grounds of Forest Hills Cemetery, this place does play quite the role in Anoka's history, including one famous ghost. The Gray Ghost, though, isn't exactly what one would imagine.

Forest Hills Cemetery. (Photo by Christy Urick.)

Forest Hills Cemetery takes up six acres in the city of Anoka referred to as "The Woods" in the late 1800s. By 1890, the city's original cemetery, Oakwood Cemetery, was beginning to fill up a little too quickly and the city decided to transform "The Woods" into Anoka's second cemetery. One rule was applied to Forest Hills Cemetery: this was to be Anoka's "nice" cemetery, so only granite grave markers were to be allowed on the grounds.

The cemetery opened for business on October 29, 1890, with the burial of Olive Stimson. Unfortunately, this was Olive's second go-round of being buried. The first time was at Oakwood Cemetery in February of 1889. Olive was disinterred from Oakwood due to overcrowding, but now has the distinction of being the first body buried in Anoka's fancier cemetery, granite grave marker and all.

Forest Hills Cemetery also serves as a military cemetery for many of Anoka's veterans. The cemetery boasts many beautiful structures and statues dedicated to our servicemen and women.

It only makes sense that a man of George Green's status and reputation would be buried in Anoka's finer final resting place. Another Anoka man held in high regard and a legend in the Anoka Halloween arena also has ties to Forest Hills Cemetery, but for a much different reason.

Olive Stimson's grave. (Photo by Christy Urick.)

Dr. William Andberg was a well-respected and much-loved veterinarian in the city of Anoka for many decades. His care and compassion for animals won over his patients and he came highly recommended to others. But Dr. Andberg's kind heart wasn't the only thing to be admired about this man. At the age of fifty-five, Dr. Andberg decided to take up running. He wanted to stay in shape and lose a little weight along the way. This little hobby turned into quite the achievement for the doctor. He set over thirty world and national records for runners in the fifty-to-ninety-year-old class of runners.

Dr. Andberg liked to train for his races inside the gates of Forest Hills Cemetery. This way he could focus on his running instead of having to worry about cars, other runners and maybe a few of his beloved K-9 patients coming to sniff him out. In 1983, Dr. Andberg was training for his hometown race. By this point in time the Anoka Halloween Grand Day Parade included a foot race for townsfolk at the start of the parade. Wearing a gray sweat suit, Dr. Andberg took off inside the cemetery on a rainy October day.

As the story goes, two elderly women were also in the cemetery that day visiting a few gravesites. As Dr. Andberg approached the women, seemingly emerging from nowhere, he gave these ladies

quite the fright. Surely, this was a ghost in gray running in the mist through the cemetery on a bleak October day. The closer Dr. Andberg got to the women, the clearer it became that he was indeed a living, breathing person, not a phantom of any sort. This story captured the imagination of those on the Anoka Halloween Committee and the race before the Grand Day Parade has been deemed the Gray Ghost 5K Run ever since.

It was a great loss for the city of Anoka and the running world when Dr. Andberg passed away in 2007, at the age of ninety-six.

The city-owned fields that lay behind Anoka High School have recently been named The Gray Ghost Fields in honor of the legendary doctor and the race that is named for him.

Seven

Patting Themselves On the Back

B Y THE MID-1920S, the Anoka Halloween Committee was so pleased with the success of the celebration they decided to throw themselves a party. Lush, lavish banquets were to be hosted at the Jackson Hotel, Anoka's finest lodging and dining establishment at the time. These banquets were to be for the Anoka Halloween Committee members and their guests, which included some of Anoka's most prominent citizens. The Jackson Hotel was happy to open its doors and elegant dining room to the committee members and their friends; it would be a nice change of pace from some of the clientele the hotel hosted during the early prohibition days of the 1920s.

Some of these guests from that era have yet to check out of the Jackson Hotel.

The Jackson Hotel, Anoka's very own grandiose hotel, was built by Swedish immigrant Charles G. Jackson in 1870. The hotel, originally known as The Anoka House, changed its official name to the Jackson Hotel around 1880. The fire of 1884 destroyed large sections of this building, causing extensive rebuilding in 1885.

1885 was also a significant year for the Jackson Hotel for another, darker reason. That year, Anoka's first murder occurred directly in front of the Jackson Hotel.

The Jackson Hotel (now Billy's Bar and Grill), 2013. (Photo by Christy Urick.)

Local man Peter Gross was having a seemingly innocent con-
versation with friend W.F. Mirick. Little did Gross know, Mirick
had spent his day drinking. At some point during this marathon
drinking session Mirick had went home to retrieve his gun. Before
Gross realized what was happening, in the middle of their conver-
sation Mirick pulled his gun on Gross and began shooting. Gross
turned to run but didn't get far before he was shot in the back by
Mirick. Gross was brought inside the Jackson Hotel by bystanders
on the street, only to die twenty hours later from his injuries in a
second-floor hotel room.

This incident did not keep the Jackson Hotel from being a destination at the turn of the century. In the 1890s, many citizens of
Minneapolis spent their Sundays taking the twenty-mile carriage
ride into Anoka for an impressive dinner at the Jackson Hotel.

The Jackson Hotel enjoyed its good reputation well into the
twentieth century. When prohibition hit in 1920, which just

happened to be the same year as Anoka's first Halloween celebration, the Jackson Hotel became a bootlegger's haven.

Legendary Minnesota gangster Tommy Banks liked to use the Jackson Hotel for his personal business. Rumor had it Tommy Banks was not only running rum out of the Jackson Hotel but a booming prostitution business, as well. It is said one of the ghosts who haunts this location today was one of Tommy's girls. This particular woman met an unfortunate end at the hand of Tommy and his gang.

Simply known as the Red-Headed Woman, this spirit of an allegedly murdered prostitute likes to make her presence known to those who come into the modern day Jackson Hotel, now known as Billy's Bar and Grill. The story of the Red-Headed Woman begins in Minneapolis. She, along with a few other working girls, were brought into Anoka by taxi cab at Tommy Banks's request for a few evenings at a time. Allegedly, the Red-Headed Woman caught the attention of the cab driver, who did quite a few of these cover-of-the-night runs for Tommy Banks. This wasn't the first time the cab driver had chauffeured this woman. Her red hair had made an impression on this young man and he thought her to be quite beautiful. He looked forward to seeing her again at the end of her stint at the Jackson Hotel.

A few nights went by and the cab driver returned to the Jackson Hotel at Tommy Banks's request to bring the women back to Minneapolis—only this time, no red-headed woman got in the cab. The other women who had been traveling with her looked shaken and upset as the piled into the back of the cab. The women remained silent during the trip back to Minneapolis. The cab driver didn't ask any questions of them, either. He seemed to have known their friend, the beautiful woman with red hair, got into a bad situation.

Tommy Banks had a reputation and pull during the prohibition era. If he wanted something to disappear, he could make it happen. Especially if that something was a body of a young woman no one may have really been looking for. A body has never been discovered in the Jackson Hotel during its many renovations, but it seems the spirit of this tragic woman remains.

The Red-Headed Woman likes to remain in the lower level of the establishment. In the basement of Billy's Bar and Grill is a cement room with only one door. This room is used for liquor storage and is kept under lock and key until it needs to be accessed by a staff member. A Billy's bartender was in the basement, as he needed to restock the bar. As he went to open the heavy door, he couldn't. After getting other staff members to help him push the door open, they discovered that cases of beer had been stacked up against the door from the inside. If a staff member were to attempt this as a prank, there would be no way for the employee to get back outside. No one was in the room.

The ice machine—covered in shiny stainless steel—for Billy's Bar and Grill is also kept in the basement. Several staff members have caught a glimpse of the reflection of a beautiful red-headed woman standing behind them.

The basement houses the manager's office of Billy's Bar and Grill, as well. During one shift, a manager was doing paperwork at the desk when all of the pagers not in use (otherwise used by servers so they can be alerted when an order for one of their tables is ready) went off at the same time, without having been activated. It seems the Red-Headed Woman was looking for a little attention.

Unexplained knocks on walls and movements in a storage closet in the basement, as well as cold spots and negative and heaving feelings are also signs the Red-Headed Woman is nearby.

She doesn't stay strictly in the basement, however. The Red-Headed Woman is also blamed for the reason not a single picture adorning the walls of the dining room of Billy's Bar and Grill remains straight. Every photo in the dining area, which are photos of Anoka's past, is crooked. At this point, the staff has thrown up their hands and no longer bothers to straighten them.

However, it seems the Red-Headed Woman has some company in the afterlife at the Jackson Hotel, a woman who seems more content helping the staff rather than hindering them.

A few years after the Red-Headed Woman seemingly slipped from the mortal coil, a woman named Emma Walker Foster worked at the Jackson Hotel as the kitchen manager. Emma Walker Foster was an African American woman holding a high ranking position at this popular destination, which was extremely rare for the time. Emma took her job very seriously and cared a great deal for the Jackson Hotel, so it would make sense Emma wanted to stay behind after she passed away in 1943.

The Jackson Hotel enjoyed decades of prominence, but as the years went on, the hotel seemed to fall out of favor as more and more people flocked to Minneapolis. The Jackson Hotel remained in operation until 1960. In the early '70s, a woman named Mary Ellen Cutter-Delong opened a French restaurant in the location after studying French cuisine, hoping to share her passion with her Anoka neighbors. The baker at this new French restaurant in town would lay out her dough for breads and pastries the night before. Early the next morning the baker would come in and get to work. As she would prepare other essentials for baking before attending to the dough, she didn't notice the dough had been kneaded and prepared for her. This happened on more than one occasion.

Unfortunately, the French restaurant didn't fare very well in meat 'n' potatoes Anoka and closed down after a short run.

Emma now seems eager to help the restaurant currently re-
siding in the Jackson Hotel. Billy's Bar and Grill has been in the
Jackson Hotel for the past two decades, and has had some help
from Ms. Emma Walker Foster along the way.

At night, after all the tables are cleared and cleaned, the chairs
are put up for the night. In the morning, the staff will come in to
already-set tables, chairs neatly tucked around them, ready for a
day's service. On some occasions, staff has come in for the day with
the coffee already brewing.

The spirit of Emma Walker Foster has also adapted to modern
times, it seems. Throughout Billy's dining room are a series of TV
sets. All but one of these television sets can be turned off via re-
motes. One server recalled an incident where she was closing up
for the night, switching off all the TVs, when she came to the one
without a remote. She climbed onto a chair to shut the set off when
the TV on the wall behind her—that had already been turned off—
switched on. Before she climbed up the chair any further, she went
to shut off the newly turned-on TV. Once that was taken care of
she turned back to climb up the chair, only to find that the remote-
less TV had already been completely unplugged for her.

The Red-Headed Woman and Emma Walker Forest are both
hesitant to leave the Jackson Hotel. These two women, who perhaps existed side by side without even crossing paths, truly gave
their lives to this location.

These two spirits keep the staff and guests at Billy's on their
toes, so much so the owners decided to never shut the lights off,
even after hours. It seems the spirits are less active when the lights
are on. Drive down Jackson Street in Anoka well after bar close and
the only lit-up location will be Billy's Bar and Grill.

P

BILLY'S BAR AND GRILL is without a doubt one of my favorite places in the city of Anoka. I have had many a night of good fun at Billy's. When my daughter's first birthday rolled around, I decided to invite everyone I knew to her party. When I quickly realized they wouldn't all fit into my house, I moved the party to Billy's Bar and Grill. What better place for a celebration than the haunted basement of a bar?

The only time I physically felt something at Billy's Bar and Grill that I couldn't explain was a few days before my daughter's birthday party. My sister and I had stopped in at Billy's to grab some lunch one afternoon and she wanted to see the basement, where the party room is located. After asking our waitress if it was okay, Cori and I went into the basement, which was dark aside from a little light at the bottom of the steps from the manager's offices.

When we reached the bottom of the staircase I felt around the corner in the dark for a light switch. While I was feeling the wall, I suddenly felt very sick to my stomach and cold. My sister, who was standing a few steps behind me, felt nothing. As soon as I was able to switch the lights on the nausea and chills went away. I can only guess I was standing in the personal bubble of a ghost. Or my lunch didn't sit right with me for a split second.

There is no denying that the party room is in the basement of a very old building: brick walls, no windows, a dampness in the air. We managed to brighten the space up a bit with some colorful balloons and festive decorations.

Knowing exactly what I was getting into having a child's birthday party in such a haunted location, I covered my bases. As my husband, stepson and I set up for the party, I made sure to take a minute and invite the ghosts—whichever ones may have been hanging out with us that particular November day—to join in the festivities with us.

Whether or not that did in fact show up to wish my Violet a happy first birthday has yet to be determined.

While not necessarily capitalizing on their spirits, the owners of Billy's Bar and Grill understand that the building has a certain appeal to curious paranormal seekers.

Billy's Bar and Grill is good enough to open their doors to community members who seek out the unknown through the unlikely channel of the city's community education program. In April of 2011, I jumped at the chance to attend a class in the basement of Billy's Bar and Grill, entitled Ghost Hunting 101.

I, along with my mother and about twenty-five other inquiring minds, sat around tables in the basement of a bar on a Monday night waiting eagerly to learn.

The class was led by two paranormal investigators, Ross and Bryan, from the Anoka Paranormal Investigators group. They were incredible, charismatic gentlemen who were very serious about their ghost hunting. The class itself was very informative. We were shown equipment and told fun facts, such as only one in three people believe in the paranormal—despite what our large class size might have led us to believe. Ross told the group, "There are ninety people upstairs who don't believe in this, who think you're crazy."

During the course of the evening the instructors went over the nuts and bolts of paranormal investigations, equipment used, types of hauntings, and so on.

Mom and I had the good fortune of sitting at a fun table. There were two self-proclaimed psychic mediums at our table, a single woman who took a shine to Mom and two dudes who decided to sign up for the class because it was "at a bar." The two psychic women at our table also happened to be ghost hunters in their own right and even brought some of their own equipment along with them to the class. When they told our table that they were sneaking in some of the own stuff, I half expected a proton pack to spill out onto the table. Not so much. The woman only had two small pieces of equipment with them.

As the class was going on, the women started to get reads on their own equipment. They seemed to be getting high EMF readings on their detector and could notice temperature changes. One of the women was wearing some kind of medical pack, on which the batteries kept draining. While this was happening, the women asked the instructors to bring over some of his equipment. Similar readings took place with the ghost hunter's equipment. One of the investigators started to take pictures of the spot, which happened to be only a few feet from my mother. Everyone in the class was getting a little excited; I even heard a few whispers of this being a set-up by the instructors to add a little more spark to the class. After a few minutes, the fervor began to die down and the readings began to dissipate. I couldn't help myself and had to snap a picture of my mom and her playing-it-cool expression during all this unexplained activity.

Later in the evening, the instructor had us listen to some EVPs—Electronic Voice Phenomenons—from an investigation they had conducted a few months prior. While our ears were tuned to the computer in the front of the room, a loud thump came from a closet my mother was sitting directly in front of, startling the entire class. Just then, the psychic women's equipment began to go crazy again.

It wasn't anything monumental, but it certainly was good fun!

Attending this class proved to me once again that Billy's is one of my favorite places in Anoka.

Billy's Bar and Grill, in the Jackson Hotel is the last stop on the Anoka County Historical Society's Ghosts of Anoka tour. It is probably one of the most memorable stops on the tour, not just because of the ghosts, but because of the sheer history that encapsulates the building.

Eight

Anoka Halloween's Bridge to the Great Depression

B Y THE END of the Roaring '20s the United States had just enjoyed one of its most prosperous decades and the citizens gladly indulged in all the riches the Jazz Age had to offer, the people of Anoka included. Unbeknownst to the populace, this era of sparkle and fun would end on a devastating note.

In 1929, construction began on a bridge, officially called the Anoka-Champlin Mississippi River Bridge but more well-known as the Ferry Street Bridge. No longer would a ferry system be required to travel between the cities of Anoka and Champlin. A dedication of the bridge was to be held in conjunction with that year's Halloween celebration.

On October 29, 1929, the New York Stock Exchange lost fourteen billion dollars in a single day. Over the course of two days, the stock market lost three hundred billion dollars, devastating the nation's economy and setting the stage for the Great Depression.

Two days later, the bridge dedication went on as planned, in grand fashion. The *Anoka Herald* brought news to the townsfolk of the dedication and Halloween celebration plans:

Stage All Set For Halloween Celebration
    Committee Met Monday and Made Final Plans
for the Many Events

Halloween Parade to Follow the Dedication Exercises to Be for the Children

Champlin school children meet at 6:30 at the school and take part in the bridge dedication. The governor is to be welcomed by a salute of seventeen guns. Commissioner E.P. Babcock will cut the ribbon opening the bridge to traffic. Indians will first cross in canoes, then comes the ferry, then horse-drawn rigs, then automobiles and then airplanes. Mrs. I.A. Coswell will break a bottle of Mississippi river water on the bridge railing and make a short speech. Then comes the fireworks and then the parade, led by the Anoka band comes to the Anoka Armory where the Halloween parade forms.

Anoka school children are the meet at the armory at 7:00 and costumes will be judges and noise-making souvenirs handed out. At 8 o'clock the parade will form and move to Jackson, to Second, to Main, to Ferry and back to the Armory.

If the weather is good, Anoka and Champlin will be hosts to twenty thousand people tomorrow evening.

These plans went off without a hitch. E.P. Babcock cut the festively colored black-and-orange ribbon that stretched across the Anoka-Champlin Bridge and the Halloween celebrations proudly marched over the Mississippi River into the new decade.

An ad in the *Anoka Union* for the bridge dedication of 1929. (Courtesy of ABC Newspaper.)

Nine

The 1930s

THE FOLLOWING DECADE of the economic depression that devastated the nation affected Anoka, but the hard times did not dampen their spirits when it came to Halloween.

The 1930s brought a series of new events to the Halloween celebration, including an activity that acted as a form of group therapy, the burning of Old Man Depression.

In fact, it seems the Great Depression didn't have any effect at all when it came to the Halloween celebrations. The first year of the decade another parade was added, this one later in the evening and dubbed the Light Up The Night parade. Parade attendees would be lit up in spectacular fashion for this late-night parade, prolonging the family events well into the night.

While the majority of American's struggled to make little food last throughout the week, the Anoka Halloween Committee introduced a pie eating contest to the festivities in 1930. There was no lack of participants.

Local merchants continued to compete for the best Halloween decorations in their storefront windows, and a vaudeville act debuted. A town sing-along now took place after the "big" parade, at Bridge Square, where a banjo player was set up.

P

Halloween Beauty Queens

A PIE-EATING CONTEST wasn't the only purely American thing the Anoka Halloween committee created in the 1930s. Another strong and steady American tradition found its way into the Anoka Halloween celebration: that of the beauty queen. This particular Anoka Halloween tradition struggled to find its footing in the early years, but is one of the most enduring events of the Anoka Halloween celebration.

In 1933, Ruth Herbold (later Moore) was seventeen when her graceful walk across the stage at Green Theater won her the title of the very first Halloween Queen, along with a small silver cup with her name inscribed on it.

No Miss Anoka was crowned again until 1947. Through restructuring of the program, this time an elementary school-aged queen and king were crowned. The queen, six-year-old Julie Moore, was the first Miss Anoka's daughter, but no one at the time made the connection. Nor did Julie's mom speak up and publicize the fact that being Miss Anoka seemed to run in the family.

After 1947, it seems the Miss Anoka program was all but suspended, only to be revived fourteen years later by local business owners. The structure this time was much more like it is today. It became a scholarship program where local businesses chose to sponsor candidates. And the candidates from now on would be young women; no more little children were to participate in the Miss Anoka pageant.

After the 1961 revival of the program, the Anoka Royalty became one of the more popular aspects of the Anoka Halloween Celebration. Today known as the Anoka Royal Ambassador Program,

Anoka Royal Ambassadors. (Courtsey of ABC Newspaper.)

this competition of sorts crowns three young women from the city of Anoka to represent the town throughout the year at celebrations in the state of Minnesota. The young women chosen are now known as "ambassadors," no longer using the terminology of "queen" or "princess," and it takes much more than a pretty smile and a graceful walk across the stage to represent Anoka these days. The scholarship program, however, has continued. The official mission statement from the Anoka Halloween website states about the program: "The Anoka Halloween Ambassador program supports the growth and development of young women in Anoka through scholarship, achievement, and grace."

2004 Anoka Royal Ambassador Megan Canny, a friend of mine, emphasizes the fact that this isn't your typical beauty pageant. "Our ability to speak and interact with people was the most important," she said. "No talent or swimsuit [competition]."

Megan also went on to talk about how a great camaraderie is formed among the contestants. "It is not a popularity contest. The

Anoka Royal Ambassadors, 2013. (Photo by Christy Urick.)

girls have no say who is crowned or who your reign with. They ask you who you get along with, but that's about it. But that is the point of the ambassador program, to band together."

The Grand Day Parade is the day the girls get to shine in their hometown, usually riding high atop a fire truck, sirens blazing.

Megan remembered that day, recounting, "We started the day at the [American] Legion, getting our hair done, since we would be going from parade appearance to the final pageant. The pre-parade reception for visiting royalty was [held] there and new candidates were there to help great us."

Playing host to visiting royalty, riding in a parade, attending a reception and coronation and smiling the entire time can take a lot out of these Halloween beauty queens, but to see them around town during the Halloween season brings a slice of Americana to the town's celebration. This is one of the reasons this tradition continues to this day.

P

Making It Official

BY 1934, ANOKA'S GRAND Halloween celebrations were becoming national news. The *Anoka Union* got letter after letter from across the nation asking about Anoka's Halloween celebrations. That year, an outdoor pillow fight and a silly kangaroo court were added to the festivities, and more people attended the dance at the Armory than any other year before.

In 1936, Anoka Halloween faced its first ever scandal. The city of Minneapolis decided to take credit for the idea of a city-wide Halloween celebration by stealing the spotlight from Anoka and mounting an enormous Halloween event. However, it seemed their lack planning was their downfall and Anoka, now old hat at whipping together a spectacular Halloween celebration, simply out-planned the City of Lakes and held a huge event that year.

The next year, 1937, Anoka made it official with the help of a very ambitious twelve-year-old boy.

P

Harold Blair:
The Paperboy Goes to Washington

Harold Blair at age twelve.
(Courtesy of ABC Newspaper.)

IN 1936, THE *MINNEAPOLIS JOURNAL* was looking for a way to boost sales. The newspaper decided to offer their paperboys an incentive: out of all the paperboys, the two hundred who sold the most issues of the daily *Minneapolis Journal* would be sent by train for a six-day trip to Washington, D.C. for a tour of the nation's capital. An Anoka boy, twelve-year-old Harold Blair, was one of the two hundred. Harold's victory did not go unnoticed by the powers that be in Anoka, especially after Minneapolis grasped for the Halloween crown a few years earlier. The city leaders planned on making Anoka the official Halloween capital and they weren't going to let Harold travel to D.C. empty-handed.

Harold was to travel by train to Washington, D.C. in February of 1937. The Commercial Club wasted no time getting to work on a few things for Harold to take with him. Drug store owner Bernard Witte decided to take the reins. He commissioned local artist Alyce Vick, who years prior created the design of the witch medallions that peppered the street of downtown Anoka, to create something for Harold to wear. Alyce came up with a patch for Harold to affix to a sweater, colored with vibrant oranges, greens, yellow and black, a witch flying over a full moon and the words "Halloween Capital" floating in the sky adjacent to the moon. A fence, open gate, and the words "The Gateway to the Great Northwest" printed across the bottom completed the patch.

Alyce's artwork couldn't be sewn on any ol' sweater of Harold's. A twelve-year-old boy during the Depression didn't exactly have clothes fit to wear to the nation's capital. Graydon Colburn, owner of the popular downtown Anoka clothing store Colburn-Hilliard and a Commercial Club member, gave Harold one of his finest yellow sweaters to wear and made sure the patch was attached properly by local tailor Mr. Moberg.

After Harold's appearance was taken care of, the Commercial Club got to work on the single paragraph that would make the city of Anoka officially The Halloween Capital of the World.

On Monday, February 22, Harold and 199 other boys boarded a private train to Washington, D.C. After a brief respite in Chicago, the train arrived in D.C. on Wednesday morning. While in D.C., the boys were lucky enough to attend a luncheon in the House of Representatives restaurant with Minnesota Representative Millard Rice. At this luncheon, Harold approached the congressman and delivered the proclamation the Commercial Club had drafted. This brief exchange between a winsome local boy and a politician in Washington, D.C. was all it took for Anoka, Minnesota, to be proclaimed The Halloween Capital of the World by Congress.

A local man, Marty Higgins, was quoted in the *Anoka Herald* in 1937 upon Harold's arrival back home, "He carried a smile so wide he could whisper in his own ear."

Harold Blair went on to be a true America hero. He joined the Navy in 1943 at the age of eighteen. Harold Blair was killed two years later aboard the U.S.S Indianapolis during the Okinawa invasion of World War II.

Unfortunately, the only thing left of the official proclamation is the envelope it arrived in addressed to Harold months after his trip.

Harold Blair's grave. (Photo by Christy Urick.)

P

THE YEAR AFTER HAROLD made his trek to Washington, D.C., a *Life* photographer made the trip to Anoka to document the festivities. Appearing in a national publication like *Life* magazine was a huge achievement for the city of Anoka and only bolstered the Halloween celebration.

The 1930s ended on a devastating note for Anoka. A tornado tore through the town in June, destroying the Anoka Armory, the building that was transformed into the grand ballroom every year for the Halloween dance. Two people were killed in the storm and several other buildings experienced severe property damage. Halloween never says "die" in the city of Anoka, however, and the parade, bonfire and other events took place as usual. The dance was moved that year to the Knights of Columbus hall and thousands still came out for the celebration

By the end of the 1930s, as the Anoka Halloween celebration approached twenty years in existence, children were being raised in a city where the Halloween importance was always there. Despite religious conviction, political affiliation or what negative things groups were saying about Halloween, the citizens of Anoka continued to hold Halloween close in their hearts, ignoring all the outside noise denouncing the holiday.

Ten

The Very First
Anoka Halloween Button

ONE OF THE STRONGEST traditions in the Anoka Halloween celebration is that of the Anoka Halloween button. Today, the
Anoka Halloween button is a design contest held for local artists.
Artwork is submitted to the Halloween committee and the winner
is chosen at the beginning of the year. The winning design is then
printed on not only buttons, as it was in the past, but on t-shirts,
sweatshirts and coffee mugs.

This all began in 1941, when Alyce Vick, who created the patch
for Harold Blair to wear to Washington, D.C. only a few years prior,
created the very first button design.

Simple and spooky, Alyce's design featured an owl perched on
a tree branch, surrounded by bats. The button itself was made out
of wood with a safety pin glued to the back.

Little did this Anoka artist realize that her idea for a cute little
keepsake for the Anoka Halloween celebration would turn into one
of the most collected items and anticipated contests that revolve
around the celebration.

Above: Anoka Halloween button collection on display in a private collection at Antiques on Main. (Photo by Olivia Dusenka.)

Left: The very first Anoka Halloween button on display in a private collection at Antiques on Main. (Photo by Olivia Dusenka.)

Eleven

Anoka State Hospital

THE ANOKA STATE ASYLUM, now known as the Anoka State Hospital, has been a part of the city of Anoka for over a hundred years, and has been included in one way or another in every Halloween celebration over the years. They even had a float in the parade every year. An unusual move for a mental institution, but their participation in the parade cemented the hospital as an undeniable part of the fabric that makes up Anoka. One year, the float was described as "outstanding in weirdness" by the *Anoka Union*. What the float exactly consisted of is unknown.

In 1949, something remarkable happened during the Anoka Halloween celebration with regard to Anoka State Hospital. The governor of Minnesota, Luther Youngdahl, was invited to the Anoka Halloween celebration. He saw this as a perfect opportunity to further his policies. Youngdahl had been governor for two years at the time of his appearance in the Halloween celebrations. In that short time, Luther Youngdahl had gained the nickname "The Sunday School Governor," as he perceived the state of Minnesota to have a gambling problem and was swift to outlaw many forms of gambling. Governor Youngdahl was also passionate about better care for the mentally ill. He had seen how those institutionalized had been subjected to terrible living conditions and barbaric forms of restraint.

Anoka State Hospital, 2013. (Photo by Christy Urick.)

As Anoka was home to one of the largest and most utilized state-owned mental hospitals, Youngdahl wrote a speech and a short program to present to the citizens of Anoka during the celebration.

After the Pumpkin Bowl halftime show, in the dark on a crisp Halloween night, in front of Anoka State Hospital and 1,000 people, with a spotlight dead-center on the governor, he delivered this speech over the hospital's loudspeaker system:

> It is just a little more than 250 years ago since mentally ill and other citizens were burned at the stake at Salem as witches.
>
> A long period of time has elapsed since then. We discarded the stake but retained in our attitudes toward the mentally ill the voodooism, demonology, fears and superstitions associated with witchcraft.

Tonight—Halloween Eve—we employ the stake and fire for another purpose, to destroy the straight-jackets, shackles and manacles which were our heritage from the Salem days.

A little as eighteen months ago all but one of our mental hospitals used mechanicals restraints. Today most are restraint-free.

The bonfire which I am lighting tonight consists of 350 straightjackets, 196 cuffs, 91 straps and 25 canvas mittens.

No patient in Anoka State Hospital is in restraint. These restraints were removed by the staff, employees and volunteer workers of the Anoka State Hospital. They were removed as the hospital's answer to witchcraft.

By this action we say more than that we have liberated the patients from barbarous devices and the approach, which these devices symbolize.

An article in the *Anoka Union* touting Governor Youngdahl at the Anoka Halloween Celebration. (Photo Courtsey of ABC Newspaper.)

With the end of the speech, Governor Youngdahl approached the pile of 673 pieces of antiquated and abusive restraints. With a torch, he set it ablaze.

P

WHENEVER I AM ON the grounds of Anoka State Hospital I feel both a rush of excitement and a pit in my stomach. I am not a psychic, medium, sensitive, seer or whatever you call someone who can feel or see the dead. I could have a ghost sitting next to me right at this minute and not have a clue. But there is a current I believe anyone can feel that cannot be explained. I feel this current the most when I am standing on the property of Anoka State Hospital.

Designed by state architect Clarence H. Johnston, Sr. (who also has the distinction of being the architect of the Glensheen Mansion in Duluth as well as many of the buildings on the University of Minnesota campus), the campus was opened by the state of Minnesota in Anoka. Originally called First State Asylum for the Insane and made up of a collection of cottages, the facility opened its doors in 1899 and was filled with patients from the overflowing asylum in St. Peter, Minnesota. By 1909, the First State Asylum became a female-only facility. In 1919, the location changed its name to the Anoka State Asylum.

While one could easily imagine the horrors that may have taken place behind the walls of the asylum in the mid-twentieth century, the reality was also filled with positives for these unwell women. While still participating in the limited science and therapies at the time, First State Asylum was one of the more humanely run mental institutions in the country. The patients were given exceptional care for the time. They were kept busy with farming, sewing and quilting, among other jobs. Along with the work, the women were seen at the on-site beauty parlor once or twice a week.

A cottage on the grounds of Anoka State Hospital, 2013. (Photo by Christy Urick.)

Manicures and facial treatments as well as shampooing were performed on the patients. Movies were also a common treat, as well as picnics and religious services.

A working farm was also on the grounds of the Anoka State Asylum. In fact, the asylum consistently turned out State Fair champion dairy cows in the early years of its existence.

This asylum still was not immune to the horrors that took place in institutions for the mentally ill in the early twentieth century. For example, it worked out that there were only two staff members per shift per 100 women—just two staff members to each cottage.

In 1920, a flu epidemic came through the facility, killing 176 patients.

In 1946, the Anoka State Asylum purchased its very first electroshock machine, making quick and frequent use of it on patients.

In 1950, the asylum became a tuberculosis center not just for the mentally ill, but for prisoners from the nearby Stillwater prison who suffered from the disease. The prisoners were all contained to a separate cottage, however. The 1950s also brought the use of tranquilizers on patients.

As the knowledge of science and medicine grew, Anoka State Asylum changed how it dealt with patients. While lobotomies, sterilizations and other barbaric practices were used on the patients at this location, these treatments changed as new information became available.

The 1970s saw a shift in focus as to what the facility was used for. It was decided that a treatment center was better suited in this area, and the mass-housed mentally ill model was phased out. The Anoka Metro-Regional Treatment center is still is use, treating those with chemical dependency on-site.

What also makes this location unique is the series of underground tunnels that run from cottage to cottage. The uses of these tunnels were numerous but they were mainly used for transferring ill patients and disposing of the deceased, taking the unclaimed bodies out through the underground tunnels to the nearby, on-site cemetery so as not to upset the other patients.

These tunnels are where the tales of most of the haunted happenings take place at Anoka State Hospital. Today, the tunnels are strictly used for security purposes, but some say desperate patients would try to escape the hospital via these tunnels.

One patient is said to have gone into the tunnels in an attempt to leave, but got so lost and turned around that she was left with no other option but to hang herself on the pipes above out of desperation.

Another tale goes that an escaped patient was making her way through the tunnels when she was caught by security, being shot on sight by the overzealous security guards.

There are also horrific stories of rape and other bodily harm coming to the patients in these tunnels.

While these stories haven't been officially confirmed, modern security guards are hesitant to check the tunnels. One said that he and his fellow guards would even play rock-paper-scissors to see who would go past a certain point on security checks because the energy in that location was so heavy and dark.

The story of the headless lady in red is also a popular tale at the Anoka State Hospital. While often spotted in the tunnels, she has also been glimpsed above ground.

Some say they have seen this woman weaving around the cottages after dark, wearing a red dress. She is believed to be the spirit of a patient who had a lobotomy performed on her while she was at the hospital.

It is unfortunate that the mentally ill people who are said to be roaming the grounds of Anoka State Hospital are forever stuck in the place that may have given them the most trouble in their tough lives.

It is important to note that no paranormal investigation group has ever been granted access to this location for a number of reasons. The property was, until very recently, owned by the state of Minnesota, who in turn has gifted it to Anoka County. This is now county-owned property; not private, but not necessarily "open to the public," and trespassing is a very arrestable offense.

Also, this is very much a working hospital. People do still reside in a few of the cottages, getting help with their chemical dependency issues. Privacy is of the utmost importance to these individuals.

In early 2013, cottages that no longer house patients found themselves in limbo. The possible destruction of these historic buildings was being considered by the county. Many people in the city of Anoka were surprised by this possibility, I being one of them. While the haunted stories of this location are many and intriguing, I believe the actual histories of the buildings are the reason they should remain standing. I spoke at the city council meeting in May of 2013 to show my support toward restoring and renovating these buildings. I gave the following speech:

> This is the first city council meeting I have ever attended, let alone the first I have ever spoken at, so I hope that shows you how much this particular topic means to me.
>
> I wanted the city council to know that there is a concern among community members in Anoka regarding the fate of the cottages on the Anoka State Hospital property.
>
> These buildings are a part of the fabric of Anoka. They speak directly to the history of the city and how much Anoka has given to the state of Minnesota when it comes to health care.
>
> Most importantly I believe, was the 1949 visit from Minnesota Governor Youngdahl to the hospital during that year's Halloween celebration. Governor Youngdahl gave a moving speech about ending the inhumane treatment of the mentally ill, a somewhat revolutionary idea for the mid-twentieth century. Governor Youngdahl chose to come to our asylum to make his point. After his speech, which echoed over the facilities loudspeakers, Governor Youngdahl lit a large bonfire made up of the horrifying restraints used on these unwell people.
>
> I could stand here and bring up the cost, the work, the environmental impact study and hazardous audit that would all have to be done before these

buildings would be demolished and all the dollar signs, negative or positive, people are seeing when this project is discussed, but I feel Governor Youngdahl's visit and the one hundred and twelve years these buildings have stood in this city are more than enough reason we should fight to save them, and I am willing to help in any way I can to defend them.

Thank you.

Many of the city council members agreed with me, one even remarking that if the cottages were to be torn down it would be like Anoka was missing a part of itself.

While I could think of a million and one uses for the cottages if they were to be restored (at the top of my list being reused for the mentally ill in a compassionate way with modern medicine, to remind ourselves how far we have come) paranormal investigations could certainly be one of them.

Since this is county-owned property, the rules and regulations would have to be many and followed to a "T," and those coming in to investigate would have to be professional and serious about what they were doing. It would be compelling and heartbreaking to get any sort of evidence of the spirits stuck on these grounds. It would be a wonderful thing if we could even somehow help release these restless spirits and help them leave the grounds of Anoka State Hospital forever.

At the same time Anoka State Hospital was attempting to come out of the dark ages, another, more lighthearted affair was started and became a proud Anoka Halloween tradition.

Anoka State Hospital Cemetery. (Photo by Christy Urick.)

Twelve

The Pumpkin Bowl
and *The Dating Game*

ONE PIECE OF AMERICANA that is one of the highlights of the Anoka Halloween celebration is that of the annual Pumpkin Bowl, a high school football game that always packs the crowd into Goodrich Field.

The Pumpkin Bowl was started just at the right time, when the Anoka Halloween celebration needed a good shot of patriotism in the form of a classic American pastime.

P

NOT ONLY DID ANOKA and the Halloween celebration see their share of struggles in the 1940s, a popular, crowd-drawing event was born that decade, a spectacle that still continues to this day.

1948 was the very first time a football game was played by Anoka High School's Tornados on the night of the Grand Day Parade. *Minneapolis Tribune* reporter Barbara Flanagan was in attendance and referred to the game as the Pumpkin Bowl in the paper the next day. The name stuck, and the game has only gained in popularity. By the 1960s, the Pumpkin Bowl was the heart and soul of the Halloween celebration.

The Anoka Halloween celebrations were highlighted on the national stage when the 1970s game show *The Dating Game* sent a winning couple—Graciela Koppers and Steve Heimple—to town for their grand prize. In 1970, the couple was flown into the Pumpkin Bowl by a helicopter that landed square in the center of Goodrich Field, where the pair was presented with a plaque by a number of high school football players.

Some couples on *The Dating Game* were sent off to exotic, warm weather destinations. This lucky couple from California got sent to Anoka, Minnesota, at the end of October.

For decades, the Pumpkin Bowl was played directly after the Grand Day Parade, but has since been moved to a more convenient Friday night during the month of October, thereby making all the Halloween merriment last even longer.

Anoka High School Football Team, 2013. (Photo by Christy Urick.)

Thirteen

Modern Halloween Celebrations

FOR THE EARLY PART of the 1950s, Anoka garnered enough national attention for Smailey Burnett, an actor under contract with Columbia Motion Pictures, to make an appearance during the Halloween celebrations.

Not to be outdone, the next year local man Dick Tollette wrote to his friend Harold Mirisch, vice president of Monogram Studios, asking for a "star" to come to the Anoka Halloween Celebration. Western actor Whip Wilson was the lucky one chosen.

In 1952, Rex Allen (another Western actor) came to town, followed by Jonny Sheffield in 1953. Tex Ritter came in 1957, thus concluding the 1950s string of celebrated Western actors coming to The Halloween Capital of the World.

The star-struck '50s gave way to the Pumpkin Bowl craze of the 1960s. The game had now become the centerpiece of the celebration, packing Goodrich Field to the brim with fans from surrounding towns to watch the Anoka Tornados take on the opposing team.

In the 1970s and '80s the celebration grew in length, expanding over nearly the entire month of October. The Halloween beauty queens now became known as ambassadors for the city of Anoka. Local businesses scrambled to sponsor a Halloween Anoka Ambassador to send to Minneapolis, St. Paul and other suburbs to

(Courtsey of ABC Newspaper.)

participate in community celebrations and parades. The Anoka Halloween committee saw to the ambassadors' float being featured in other town's civic celebrations, poising each ambassador with a costume and a smile on top of the float.

To this day the Grand Day Parade is *the* draw of the Anoka Halloween celebration. This parade now holds the title of Minnesota's largest, longest-running parade. Thousands upon thousands of people come into town for the Grand Day Parade, now held on the Saturday prior to October 31. Schools, community organizations, political candidates and more marching bands than you can count take over Main Street rain, snow or shine.

Early days of the Grand Day Parade. (Courtsey of ABC Newspaper.)

Children of all ages take part in the festivities. (Courtsey of ABC Newspaper.)

The Anoka Grand Day Parade takes place rain or shine (Photos courtesy of ABC Newspaper.)

Fourteen

The Grand Day Parade

Thousands of people come into town for the Grand Day Parade, Minnesota's largest and longest-running parade. While those participating in the parade plan for months and weeks getting their floats just right and their dance routines and costumes perfected, those gunning for a spectator spot on the parade route start the night before.

My aunt Carla's house is blocks from the end of the parade route. During my childhood we claimed a corner right at the end

Spectators turn out in droves for the Grand Day Parade. (Photo by Christy Urick.)

An Anoka High School student gets a prime spot on the Anoka Halloween parade route. (Photo by Christy Urick.)

of the parade for our family, but that claiming took work. The night before, our family, along with the other folks in the know in the city of Anoka, took lawn chairs and blankets and laid claim to spots on the Grand Day Parade route.

Our spot has since changed, due to the growth of our families and friends, but we still claim our new spot in the same fashion. We tend to tie our lawn chairs together, though, just to make sure.

At my aunt's house and now at my sister's house, it is like an early Christmas for my family. We all make a dish to share before and after the parade (usually something warm and delicious) and enjoy each other's company, excited that it's parade day.

If you drive down Main Street the morning of the parade and see all the empty chairs and blankets, some surrounded by fake police tape, it looks as though a parade was taking place when all the people suddenly disappeared.

P

DESCRIBING THE DAY of the Anoka Halloween parade brings out the poet in me. I can't remember ever missing a year. I have taken days off of work to make sure I am in my lawn chair on Main Street wearing layers of clothing, covered in a blanket, breathing in the cold air and taking it all in.

Watching the children, my own included, dive for the candy makes me feel like a child again. Halloween is such an incredible time of year, and at that moment in time for those kids, it's all about the candy.

Anoka Halloween Parade, 2013. (Photo by Christy Urick.)

I love watching the marching bands, the folksy handmade floats from towns all over Minnesota and the local kids so proud to be walking down the street in this historic parade.

The end of October in Minnesota can bring any sort of weather. Remember 1991? I can only remember one year where the weather for the parade was less than ideal. It rained and snowed on and off during the parade, but it didn't matter—the crowds still came out in droves. Every other year it has always been a sun-soaked fall day, as it deserves to be.

Anoka Halloween Parade, 2013. (Photo by Christy Urick.)

Last year, I stood on the sidewalk as the parade ended and I thought about how much I loved this seemingly silly tradition. My heart was full. The Grand Day Parade is a mix of two things I am very passionate about, Halloween and the city of Anoka. It's like this day was made just for me.

P

While the Anoka Halloween Celebration seems about as American and innocent as Grandma's apple pie cooling on a windowsill, it has not been without its pitfalls. Nothing can go on for almost one hundred years and not have some sort of controversy pop up every now and then.

Marching in an October rainstorm. (Courtesy of ABC Newspaper.)

Fifteen

Halloween Tragedy and Controversy

ASIDE FROM THE BRIEF tussle with the city of Minneapolis in the 1930s over the Halloween Capital of the World title, the Anoka Halloween celebrations have been without much controversy.

The Halloween Committee has been made up of fair-minded, enthusiastic people who love their city and their neighbors and have tried their best to put on the best Halloween celebration possible. But when something has been around as long as the Anoka Halloween celebration, keeping the record completely spotless is nearly impossible.

Only two things have occurred since the 1930s that blemish the nearly perfect record for flawless Anoka Halloween celebrations. The first was an incident beyond the committee's (or anyone else's) control, and the second was a decision made by the Halloween committee that made national news for all the wrong reasons.

P

1961 Children's Parade

IN 1961, NOT SO MUCH a controversy but a downright tragedy occurred at the Big Parade of Little People, the parade held for Anoka's costumed schoolchildren the day before the Grand Day Parade .

At 11:00 a.m. that day, 4,000 kids from Anoka, Coon Rapids and Champlin were let out of their classrooms to partake in a few fun activities before lining up on Main Street in their Halloween costumes. They would begin to march in their very own parade at precisely 1:15 p.m.

Things began without a hitch. The children marched and the people on the street cheered them on. At 2:34 p.m. seventy-six-year-old Otto Erickson was bringing his wife, Lena, to a doctor's appointment several blocks away from the children's parade. He dropped her off at the clinic and from there somehow drove closer to the parade route, ran a red light and careened onto Main Street, hitting a group of sixth graders toward the end of the parade as well as several spectators. Two people were killed by Otto Erickson's vehicle. Erickson himself was also discovered to be dead by the time the police got to him, a victim of a heart attack. Seven others were severely injured, including four children.

Despite this horribly occurrence, the Anoka Halloween celebrations continued throughout the remainder of the week.

Anoka Union headline from the 1961 Big Parade of Little People. (Courtesy of ABC Newspaper.)

P

Justin's Gift

IN 2012, THE ANOKA Halloween Committee found itself embroiled in a controversy that reached a fever pitch of local and national media coverage the committee could never have imagined.

An Anoka/Champlin-based youth support group for lesbian, gay, bi-sexual, transgender and questioning youth and their allies called Justin's Gift applied to march in the Anoka Halloween Grand Day Parade. The Anoka Halloween Parade has always been welcoming to the gay community, having had several groups representing different aspects of the LBGTQ community march in the past.

This particular group, Justin's Gift, was born out of a tragedy that occurred within the city of Anoka. In 2009 and 2010, the Anoka-Hennepin school district had a suicide epidemic among its

students. The children who killed themselves were either gay or perceived to be gay by their peers at school. Incessant bullying of these kids occurred and this was one of the factors that played a role in their suicides. These suicides and the bullying were so shocking and happened in such large numbers that the problem was covered by CNN and *Rolling Stone*, among other national media outlets.

Justin's Gift logo. (Courtesy of Justin's Gift.)

Justin Aaberg was one such

child who saw no other way out of his situation. The ninth grader at Anoka High School had recently come out as gay. While his family and friends accepted Justin and loved him regardless of his sexual orientation, he was met with physical assault and damaging emotional and mental abuse at school by his classmates. Justin committed suicide on July 9, 2010, after a series of text messages to a friend about his difficulties at school.

Justin's family wanted to give back after the loss of their son and decided to create the Justin's Gift organization for kids like him and those who supported these kids right here in Anoka and Champlin. The group found success and support in the community and flourished.

Walking in the Anoka Halloween Grand Day Parade is a logical step for a successful organization in the community to take, and Justin's Gift was no different. The adults in charge wanted the kids to experience the joy and excitement of walking in this huge, historic parade. It seemed all deadlines were met and all the paperwork was in order. The group was denied entrance. The reason given was that the parade was "full."

In any other year, in any other town, this would have been an understandable reason, but 2012 was an election year. And not just any election year, but a contentious one. Like most things, even a parade can be made into a political statement. The news media got a hold of this story (it is important to note that this did not come from the Justin's Gift people) and it became quite explosive, covered for days in local media and touched upon at a national level as well.

Anoka, while being a fairly politically independent city itself, resides in a congressional district which is among the most conservative in the state of Minnesota. People were crying foul on the exclusion of Justin's Gift, calling the decision a comment by the Anoka Halloween Committee on on the gay rights movements occurring in the state.

At first, the benefit of the doubt was given to the Halloween Committee. The fair-minded people of Anoka wanted to see the facts and hear from the committee itself before drawing any conclusions. As the days went on, the Anoka Halloween Committee remained silent. No local media could seem to get a hold of them. No interested citizen, myself included, could get a response from them. It seemed the committee was just waiting for this media storm to be over.

It can be argued that the Anoka Halloween Committee doesn't have to answer for the decisions it makes when it comes to who can and cannot walk in the Grand Day Parade. The Halloween Committee remains a non-profit, volunteer-run organization like it has always been, but the committee has a responsibility to the city of Anoka and all of its townspeople. George Green understood that. He did all he could to include everyone in the city of Anoka during the Halloween celebrations. Inclusion has always been at the forefront of this celebration, and that is what makes it so much fun.

Justin's Gift still had a presence at the 2012 Grand Day Parade. The organization had a booth set up in the parking lot of a church on the parade route where they sold t-shirts, buttons, bracelets and other items. Floats from other cities also showed their solidarity with the group by mounting signs next to their waving princesses that read, "We Support Justin's Gift."

In my opinion, it is unfortunate that the Anoka Halloween Committee handled this situation in such graceless manner. One can only hope they have learned from this mistake and not only make more informed decisions in the future but also realize that even though they are an autonomous organization, they are representing something very special in this city. When a question is asked, an answer should be waiting.

Justin's Gift was able to proudly walk among its community members in the 2013 Anoka Halloween Parade. The group was met with cheers and support from onlookers.

Justin's Gift walks in the 2013 Anoka Halloween Parade. (Photo By Christy Urick.)

Sixteen

Identity
and
Party Papers & Costumes

THE ANOKA HALLOWEEN CELEBRATION defines Anoka to many people outside of the city. The citizens of Anoka take pride in it. The city flourishes or flounders on how the Halloween celebration turns out any given year. The entire city takes a hit when a poor decision is made by the Halloween Committee and the entire city beams with pride when a wonderful decision is made by the Halloween Committee. For better or for worse, Halloween and this celebration is Anoka's identity.

As former Anoka mayor Bjorn Skogquist stated in July 2012, "From a standpoint of identity, every small town has their festival, and this is ours and it happens to be really big."

Witch medallion by City Hall. (Photo by Christy Urick.)

Promotional materials for the City of Anoka. (Courtsey of ABC Newspaper.)

It is only natural that a city with such a strong Halloween identity as Anoka has one of the best costume shops in the state of Minnesota. Not only is Party Papers & Costumes the premier costume shop in The Halloween Capital of the World, it is also the place I have called my part-time home for the last six years. You could say Party Papers & Costumes is where I got my start as The Halloween Honey.

Party Papers and Costumes is proud to carry on Anoka's Halloween traditions, but the shop also carries on another strong Anoka tradition: hauntings.

P

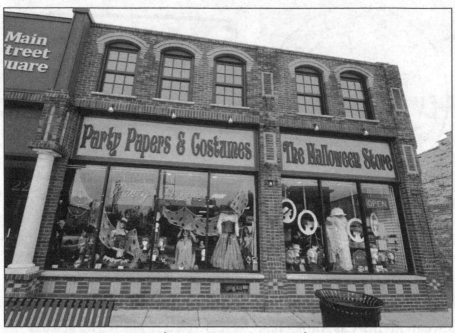

Party Papers & Costumes. (Photo by Chrisy Urick.)

"Devote Your Life to Halloween"
Party Papers & Costumes

A COSTUME SHOP in The Halloween Capital of the World is held to a certain standard, and Anoka's very own independent costume shop, Party Papers & Costumes more than reaches the standard expected. An amazing costume selection, a dynamic staff that is knowledgeable about make-up, hair and costuming trends, and a tireless owner who is passionate about all things Halloween are absolute musts when operating The Halloween Store in The Halloween Capital of the World. Having a ghost or two seems as natural as breathing.

Party Papers & Costumes is lucky enough to have some extra help all year long that isn't on the payroll, and who aren't necessarily of the physical world. The building Party Papers & Costumes

The Main Street Square building. (Photo by Christy Urick.)

calls home, 222 East Main Street, in the Main Street Square building, predates Anoka's Halloween Capital title by five years. Built in 1916 by the man behind Halloween himself, George Green, along with his father Clarance, the first business to occupy this space was Price Confectionary.

Sweets seemed to be the business of choice for 222 East Main Street in the building's early years. Shortly after Price Confectionary, Clements Confectionary moved in. However, in 1921, Main Motors Sales Company was born and in 1922, the space Party Papers & Costumes now occupies became the Main Motors showroom.

In the 1990s, long after Main Motors had moved to its current location off Highway 10 in Anoka, several other business moved in and out of 222 East Main Street, until Party Papers & Costumes moved there permanently in 1994. The shop's owner, Mary, is more in tune to the otherworldly than most, and that's when the supernatural activity started to gain some attention.

It is said that two ghosts haunt this shop, from two separate eras. A male shopkeeper, who seems to be more of a residual haunting, has been seen by psychics as constantly sweeping his store. His innocent housekeeping duties are causing problems for the current store, though. The front of Party Papers & Costumes is dedicated to the party shop. Napkins, plates, and decorations for all occasions, as well as greeting cards and gift shop merchandise occupy this large space. This was where the first unexplained occurrences took place.

The napkins displayed neatly and orderly along the side wall occasionally fall to the ground, knocked down by an invisible force. The gift merchandise suddenly finds itself in a different location from where it started, but no customer has been browsing.

When this shopkeeper was the occupant of the space the streets of Anoka were much, much wider. All the lumber from the mills had to been brought through town with horse and cart. The sidewalks then were also much wider. When the streets were narrowed to keep up with the changing times, the sidewalks came in with them. The front of the Main Street Square building was expanded and the front of the store now occupies the space where the original sidewalk was. This spirit is still sweeping the sidewalk, unaware that he is upsetting the modern-day merchandise.

It is the female ghost in the costume area of the shop—the entire back part of the store—that is said to be the wicked one, in the most maternal way possible. Believed to be from an even earlier era, perhaps a time before the building was even built, she is a bit protective of the staff, even when playing a scary prank on them. Wigs high up on display shelves secured to wig blocks have been sent sailing to the occasional rude customer, narrowly missing them as they exit. Full makeup displays have been seemingly thrown to the floor after a customer complained of not finding what they needed and making a fuss.

This particular spirit likes to play with the Halloween props as well. For example, she once ably removed a carefully hung stack of plastic butcher knives and hid them under a nearby Grim Reaper robe for the staff to find in the morning. Needless to say, the employees found this a bit unsettling.

P

IN THE SIX YEARS I have been employed at Party Papers & Costumes, I have experienced some unexplained yet harmless mischief. But something occurred this past spring made me a true believer in the ghosts of Party Papers.

I was working on a Thursday night. When we are at work, we oftentimes don't even think about the ghosts. We keep busy help-ing customers or working on store projects, and only really stop to think about the ghosts when they want some attention.

That night I was in the basement, in our stockroom. Our stockroom is made up of a long, narrow, locked room within the larger basement area. I opened the door to put back an overstock of Mardi Gras beads, kept in cardboard boxes right inside the stockroom. I didn't even have to step in the room to put the extras away.

Right outside the doorway is a long wardrobe rod used to hang the longer Halloween decorations. On that Thursday night a single Halloween decoration hung on the wardrobe rod: a pumpkin-head ghost with long, flowing fabric hanging down. I've seen this deco-ration a million times. He'd been down there since November and wouldn't come back up until August or so. I looked directly at him as I opened our stockroom door and fully expected to see him as I turned to shut the door and walk back into the basement proper. As I turned to shut the door behind me, standing right in front of me was not the Halloween decoration, but what appeared to be a person. At first blush, I thought it was the shop's owner, Mary. Mary is a small woman with short black hair and happened to be wearing a white-collared shirt that day—something very similar to what this apparent person looked like and was wearing. You know those split seconds it takes your brain to process? My brain processed,

"Hey, that's not Mary. I heard no one else come down the steps, and I am down here alone."

This entity had the same short black hair and white-collared shirt on as Mary did, but he was young man. Ten or so, I'd say, and wearing what I can only describe as a black dinner jacket over his shirt. I turned my head away, after all those wires connected in my brain and I realized I was looking at something that shouldn't be there. By the time I turned my head back, he was gone. In his place hung my little pumpkin-head Halloween decoration. I stood for a split second, then I moved into action. Those basement doors locked, the light switched flipped and I ran up those creaky old stairs faster than I had in a long time. My heart was nearly beating out of my chest when I got back to the shop. There stood Mary, along with our co-worker Jess. I told them what happened. They both were pleased that one of our spirits decided to show himself to me.

I was a little unsettled, since we've always assumed the ghosts in our shop were a male and a female, and both older. So to see something that was definitely a child not of this mortal plane was a bit upsetting.

Since this happened early in my shift, I eventually calmed down and went about my business again, steering clear of the basement the rest of the night.

I wasn't afraid of this apparition I saw; I was just surprised, let's say.

Luckily for the staff of Party Papers & Costumes, the spirits that have been left behind have a great deal of respect for us, or so it seems. When an employee who had worked at Party Papers & Costumes full-time for several years came back to visit after being away for a while, she was greeted in raucous style.

A large box of industrial garbage bags are kept tightly against the wall of the staircase heading into the store's other basement stockroom, this one directly below the store. As this former employee was happily gabbing with her former co-workers, a large noise was heard from the basement, as if someone had fallen down the steps. The owner rushed to check. No one was hurt. The large box of garbage bags had just been sent sailing down the steps, as if the ghosts were trying to say "Hello" to a friend.

In the basement long after the shop has closed at night, footsteps can be heard above, as well as voices coming from the back of the building. It seems Halloween and the celebrations that surround it in the city of Anoka really bring out the spirits' playful sides at Party Papers & Costumes.

The ghosts don't limit themselves to contact just with the staff of Party Papers & Costumes, however. A small office in the back of the building, tucked far away from the store, is rented by a local night-owl attorney. One night during the last Halloween season, he heard some commotion up in the front of the building. Being it was late and all the businesses had long been closed, he decided to check it out just to be on the safe side. He made his way toward the front of the building, where Party Papers & Costumes is located. The staff had hung two of the large pumpkin-headed ghost decorations on the outside of the shop door in the hall. He reached the decorations and heard another loud noise directly behind him. The attorney whipped around to face what was behind him, but nothing was there. He turned back around and the pumpkin-headed ghost decorations were whirling frantically in a circle. Needless to say, the attorney stayed in his office the remainder of the night.

Party Papers & Costumes is a featured stop of the Anoka County Historical Society's Ghosts of Anoka tour, naturally.

It's also one of the most popular destinations in the city of Anoka during the Halloween celebrations, not only because of its

Party Papers employees get into the Halloween spirit year-round. (Photo by Christy Urick.)

rich haunted history but because of its reputation for having some of the best costumes in the state of Minnesota.

P

TODAY, ANOKA'S IDENTITY is Halloween. But before the Halloween celebrations even began, the town's identity lay in the town's groundbreaking citizens.

The Doctors Alanson and Flora Aldrich only lived to see one Anoka Halloween celebration, but their spirits live on in this city, giving The Halloween Capital of the World not only two amazing people to call our own, but some of the best ghost stories in town.

Seventeen

Colonial Hall

TWO OF ANOKA'S MOST prominent citizens only lived to see their beloved city celebrate Halloween in its grand style one year, the first year in 1920. They passed away before the city of Anoka would claim to be The Halloween Capital of the World. But this doctor and his wife (who later became a physician in her own right), transplants from Massachusetts, were drawn to the city in the same way Halloween was.

Colonial Hall. (Photo by Christy Urick.)

Dr. Flora Aldrich. (Courtesy of ABC Newspaper.)

In the heart of Anoka, off Main Street on the corner of Third and Monroe sits a grand, Greek revival-style home. Impressive pillars frame the front entrance. This seventeen-room house, built in 1904, was used for more than just a luxurious home for two doctors from out east. Dr. Alanson Aldrich and his wife, Flora Aldrich, came to Anoka on their honeymoon in 1879, to visit friends. The couple was so taken with the city they decided they wanted to stay on a permanent basis.

The Doctors Aldrich were quite a coup for the city of Anoka. While the city had several of its own homegrown citizens of note, they had none quite like Dr. Flora Aldrich.

Born in New York, Dr. Flora Aldrich married Dr. Alanson Aldrich at the age of seventeen in his home state of Massachusetts. After moving to Anoka, Flora decided to pursue her dream of becoming a doctor alongside her husband. She attended the University of Minnesota College of Medicine, receiving her degree in March of 1887, at the age of twenty-one. Dr. Flora Aldrich would become the first female doctor from Anoka. She even received congratulations from the local paper, the *Anoka Union,* in February of that year:

> Mrs. Dr. A.G. Aldrich secured the first prize, a very fine Laryngascope, last week, at the Minneapolis Hospital college, for passing the best examination on diseases of the throat and lungs. Mrs. Aldrich will

graduate next month, and will then practice in Anoka. The *Union* wishes her unlimited success.

A three-room suite on the upper level of their home functioned as Dr. Flora's practice. She saw mostly women and children in her home clinic, while her husband kept a medical practice in Minneapolis. The Aldriches wanted to make sure they, as well as their patients, were comfortable in this home clinic. All the modern conveniences were installed in the house, including, according to the Anoka County Historical Society, a "hot water heating plant, a laundry, cold storage room and a fuel room. The house was fitted with all the needed call bells and connections. Two telephones, two bathrooms and electric lights were also installed in this ideal home." It is said to have been the most modern home in Anoka for the time.

Aside from being a doctor, Dr. Flora Aldrich was also a successful writer. She published three books in her lifetime, including *My Child and I*, a book for new mothers, *The Boudoir Companion*, a book for women regarding sexual health, and a novel she dedicated to her husband, *The One Man*, all written at her beloved Colonial Hall.

In a time long before tabloids or reality television, the goings-on of the Doctors Aldrich made for good gossip in the small town they lived in. The *Anoka Union* was often quick to report on what the Aldriches were up to when not treating patients. One such example comes from May 28, 1913:

> Drs. Aldrich have purchased a handsome new automobile, and when Mrs. Dr. Aldrich drives the car Dr. Aldrich holds on for dear life.
>
> (*Anoka Union*)

The Aldriches were popular, well-respected people in the city of Anoka. They opened their home to their fellow community members not just for medical treatments but for community events ,as well. It is said the Colonial Hall was used for weddings and other grand occasions for Anoka's other well-to-do citizens.

P

ON MARCH 21, 1921, Dr. Flora Aldrich passed away at her beloved Colonial Hall at the age of fifty-five.

From the *Anoka Union*, March 21, 1921, comes the following report:

> Friends of Dr. F.L.S. Aldrich were pained and shocked to hear of her sudden death which occurred Saturday noon. Her friends had known that she had not been well for a long time and that she was contemplating a trip away for rest and quiet but they did not deem her condition quite so serious. A few weeks ago, she had taken two weeks rest in bed but had again resumed seeing some of her patients. She had not been sleeping well nights and had told her maid who slept near that if she was sleeping in the morning, not to disturb her as she needed the rest. When the maid, fearful lest she was ill, tried to arouse without any results, she became alarmed and summoned friends nearby. Physicians were difficult to locate but Dr. Crowley and Dr. Wheat reached her bedside as she was breathing her last.
>
> Her brother, in the east, notified Anoka friends that he would arrive here probably Tuesday and

funeral services will be held from the home at two
o'clock today. Rev. A.D. Stowe will officiate.

Dr. Alanson Aldrich passed away only a few short months after
his wife. They doctors left behind no children, but several hunting
dogs.

Since there were no heirs to the property, the city of Anoka
took over the deed and attached the city's Masonic Lodge to Colonial Hall. Eventually the home became the offices of the Anoka
County Historical Society. When the historical society grew and
needed additional space, they moved out. Now Colonial Hall is
home to the The Artique, an antique and art gift shop.

P

PEOPLE WHO WORKED FOR the Anoka County Historical Society and
the staff at The Artique are privy to the hauntings inside Colonial
Hall. In fact, the Anoka County Historical Society has made this
stop one of the highlights of their annual Ghosts of Anoka Tour.

Since Dr. Flora Aldrich did pass away in this location, it is very
possible the spirit that remains is hers. Some have claimed to see
the figure of a woman looking down at them from a second-floor
window overlooking the front entrance.

It seems unexplainable happenings can occur anywhere in this
building. Employees and customers alike at The Artique have experienced what feels like someone brushing up against them or
touching their arm when no one is around. A sensation of being
followed on the upper levels, where Dr. Flora's clinic was, is also a
common feeling.

Dr. Alanson Aldrich had affection for a good cigar. Some have
claimed to smell cigar smoke while in the building, when smoking
has been banned for several decades in this building.

The Aldriches' hunting dogs are also said to have made an appearance at modern-day Colonial Hall. A darting vision out of the corner of the eye, which can only be explained as some kind of dog, has been seen by more than one person.

When the historical society called this location home, they had several displays set up recalling Anoka County's past. One such display was on the upper level of the home. A woven basket filled with balls of yarn, with knitting needles stuck in one of the balls, stood on display. One employee often noticed that the carefully placed knitting needles occasionally ended up on the floor. For a while this was chalked up to careless visiting school groups or other people knocking them off, until it became almost consistent. One evening, this employee decided to test her theory. She took the knitting needles and buried them under all the balls of yarn in the basket and left for the night. Sure enough, when she came back the next morning the needles had been thrown to the floor. Dr. Flora Alrdrich, it seems, was making a statement about knitting.

P

AN INTERESTING ELEMENT was added to Colonial Hall when the antique shop moved in. It seems this gave Dr. Flora more to play with, or she has some company that happens to be attached to some of the objects for sale.

One story is that in the lower level of Colonial Hall, where more of the bigger antiques are kept, a large dresser with a tall mirror bolted to the dresser had come in. The staff settled the piece of furniture downstairs and left for the evening. When they came back in the morning, an employee went into the basement to check things out, and found that the mirror had been unbolted from the dresser and laid mirror-side up on the floor next to the dresser.

There was no way of explaining any of this, since not only would unbolting the mirror and moving it to the floor have been at least a two-person job, but no one was in the building after close and the dresser and mirror had been left intact.

P

THE GHOST STORIES aren't left to just Colonial Hall alone. The Masonic Lodge attached to the home seems to experience some spillover haunting as well. A maintenance worker one night thought he was alone in the lodge, cleaning up after a meeting. He then noticed a man go into the bathroom. He waited a while before he decided to enter the bathroom to tell the gentleman that he was not to be in the building after hours, but as he went to confront the man, there was no one in the bathroom but himself.

P

IT'S NO WONDER THAT Dr. Flora Aldrich, a woman who has made such an impact on the city of Anoka, would be in no hurry to leave. She loved the city and her home so very much. Perhaps so much so that she still considers herself very much the lady of the house.

Eighteen

Tell No Tales

I HAVE ONLY TOLD a few of the haunted tales that take place in the Halloween Capital of the World. These certainly aren't the only ones, just some of the best known.

Around every corner in Anoka is another haunted location. The ghosts of Anoka's past aren't in a hurry to leave. There are countless private homes in this city, with stories I have heard firsthand, that are without a doubt haunted. They are the spirits of those who came before Anoka was The Halloween Capital of the World, possibly even before Anoka was a city, along with the spirits of some of Anoka's more modern citizens.

You can certainly believe that Billy's Bar and Grill, The Artique and Party Papers & Costumes aren't the only haunted businesses in this town, either. Go up and down Main Street, stop in for a chat, and you will surely be told a ghost story or two. That is, if the store's owners want people to know about it.

With the popularity of the paranormal on the rise, people are becoming less afraid to speak out about the unexplainable things that happen in their lives. I think this, too, is the reason Anoka is becoming such a haunted destination. More stories are being told, more research and investigating is going into them and people are learning the truth behind the hauntings in the Halloween Capital.

While the connections between Anoka being The Halloween Capital of the World and one heck of a haunted city aren't direct, they are certainly there. That supernatural current that runs through the town—the one that makes the city so desirable for ghosts—also made Anoka The Halloween Capital of the World.

An Anoka Halloween Banner on a streetlight. (Photo by Christy Urick.)

Nineteen

Why Would You Want to Leave?

WHETHER YOU BELIEVE in ghosts or not, it is truly undeniable there are spirits who stay behind in this town. Anoka is filled with generations of families who have never left and have no intention of leaving. People move to this town and feel drawn here, never to move outside the city limits again. Anoka is somewhat of a magnet for those who call this town home, me included. I have always felt a connection to this small piece of land and I don't have any intention of leaving now that I am here.

It may be the calming rivers that surround Anoka like a comforting arm around the shoulder. It may be the vibe of a bygone era of Main Street, the small businesses and the proud homes that keep people here or it just may be something else. It may be the land beneath our feet. It may be the water. It may be the history. An unexplainable reason may be the answer as to why so many of Anoka's residents are hesitant to leave, even after their physical bodies have given out and only the spirit remains. The town of Anoka has proven itself to be nothing if not full of boundless energy—from the people, from the land, from the rivers.

George Green, Harold Blair and the rest of Anoka's citizens harnessed this energy and made Anoka into the thing it was always destined be, The Halloween Capital of the World. The Doctors

Aldrich, The Jacksons, the tireless nurses and doctors at the asylum continued to harness the energy that runs through Anoka to do great things, bring joy and ease suffering to thousands of lives. The employees and business owners who open their doors every day to the city as well as the steadfast citizens who call Anoka home still harness that palpable energy today. It is a dynamic city, rich in history. Sharing the town's history is what makes this energy continue to flow. The supernatural current flows so strongly because of the people who came before us. Some may choose to stay, some may have no choice but to stay, but Anoka knows they are here.

And what better place to haunt than Anoka, Minnesota: The Halloween Capital of the World?

Main Street in downtown Anoka. (Photo by Christy Urick.)

Myself—hanging by the famous witch medallion in downtown Anoka. (Photo by Christy Urick.)

Acknowledgments

I ALWAYS KNEW THESE stories were there. It was just a matter of figuring out how to tell them.

I couldn't have figured out this book without a massive amount of help, starting with the City of Anoka itself. My spooky little town serves as a daily inspiration to me, in every aspect of my life.

This book would be many blank pages without the help of the Anoka County Historical Society and their knowledgeable, friendly staff and volunteers, especially Elaine, Todd and Darlene for digging around in the archives, sharing stories with me and lending an ear when I just needed to ramble.

I want to thank the owner of Party Papers & Costumes, Mary Vander Laan. I am fortunate enough to not only have worked for this remarkable woman for seven years, I am proud to call her my friend. Mary's encouragement in this project was immense and every time I spoke to her about the book she would re-ignite the fire which occasionally waned when I was working on this project by sharing her stories, experiences and advice. I value her presence in my life and am so lucky to have someone of her caliber on my side. She would call me a great cheerleader for Anoka all the while she was being a great cheerleader for me.

My family and friends offered me endless support and encouragement while working on this project. Not only my husband Jim but my children, Quinn and Violet, as well. Even though they are just kids they knew that when I was "working" on my laptop at home, I was, like, really working. They understood and respected my space and time and for that I am eternally grateful to them.

However, it did take A LOT of people to help me when it came to the kids during the writing process. To my mom, Debbie; to my mother-in-law, Vickie; my aunt Beth; my sister, Cori; my brother-in-law, Derek; and even HIS mom, Pam Sebesta: your time contributed to my time and all our time is precious, so I thank you all so much for giving up slices of yours to be there as a caregiver for my young daughter.

The beautiful photos, cover and additional artwork throughout this book would not be something I could ever achieve. I am beyond blessed to have such amazingly talented friends and family to contribute to the visuals of this book. Christy Urick's photographs and Kristi Carlson's designs are more beautiful than I could ever imagine for this book. Olivia Dusenka's photographic contributions to this project are breathtaking and I am so proud to be able to share this book with all three of you. It truly has become "our" book.

A huge thank you to the Twin Cities Paranormal Society and Anoka Paranormal Investigations for helping me get it right when it came to ghosts. I may watch the shows and read the books, but to be exposed to firsthand accounts of the paranormal was invaluable and added so much to this project.

My friend and fellow author Brian Landon, for his advice and never complaining once for having to listen to my mini freak-outs and meltdowns.

And to North Star Press on the goat farm in St. Cloud! I would have been a little leery of you people if a black cat didn't sit in on our meetings.